BRIDGES
TO GRACE

Evan
Sanderson

The Leadership Network Innovation Series

The Big Idea: Aligning the Ministries of Your Church through Creative Collaboration, Dave Ferguson, Jon Ferguson, and Eric Bramlett

Confessions of a Reformission Rev.: Hard Lessons from an Emerging Missional Church, Mark Driscoll

Deliberate Simplicity: How the Church Does More by Doing Less, Dave Browning

Ethnic Blends: Mixing Diversity into Your Local Church, Mark DeYmaz and Harry Li

Leadership from the Inside Out: Examining the Inner Life of a Healthy Church Leader, Kevin Harney

The Monkey and the Fish: Liquid Leadership for a Third-Culture Church, Dave Gibbons

The Multi-Site Church Revolution: Being One Church in Many Locations, Geoff Surratt, Greg Ligon, and Warren Bird

A Multi-Site Church Road Trip: Exploring the New Normal, Geoff Surratt, Greg Ligon, and Warren Bird

Servolution: Starting a Church Revolution through Serving, Dino Rizzo

Sticky Church, Larry Osborne

The Surge, Pete Briscoe with Todd Hillard

Dangerous Church, John Bishop

Other titles forthcoming

BRIDGES TO GRACE

Innovative Approaches to Recovery Ministry

Liz Swanson & Teresa McBean

ZONDERVAN®
.com

Leadership �֍ Network
Innovation Series

ZONDERVAN.com/
AUTHORTRACKER
follow your favorite authors

ZONDERVAN

Bridges to Grace
Copyright © 2011 by Liz Swanson and Teresa McBean

This title is also available as a Zondervan ebook. Visit www.zondervan.com/ebooks.

This title is also available in a Zondervan audio edition. Visit www.zondervan.fm.

Requests for information should be addressed to:

Zondervan, *Grand Rapids, Michigan 49530*

Library of Congress Cataloging-in-Publication Data

Swanson, Liz.
    Bridges to grace : innovative approaches to recovery ministry / Liz Swanson
and Teresa McBean.
        p. cm. — (The leadership network innovation series)
        ISBN 978-0-310-32967-1 (softcover)
        1. Church work with recovering addicts. 2. Church work — United States.
I. McBean, Teresa. II. Title.
BV4460.3.S93   2011
259'.429—dc22   2011007876

Cover design: *Jeff Gifford*
Interior design: *Matthew Van Zomeren*

Printed in the United States of America

11 12 13 14 15 16 /DCI/ 22 21 20 19 18 17 16 15 14 13 12 11 10 9 8 7 6 5 4 3 2 1

This book is dedicated to Tom and Patricia Chambers
in appreciation for their investment
in the ministry of recovery and their belief in me.
And to my daughter, Kacey,
whose life brings me so much joy
and who is the answer to a prayer
I prayed twenty-five years ago.
— Liz

I'd like to dedicate this book to my family:
my DNA family of Joneses and McBeans,
who make life so spicy and rich;
my small group sisters;
and the family God has provided through less traditional means—
those of us who have bonded together through suffering,
seeking, and solving problems as we learn together
how to find the life God intended for us.
I pray that I honored the spirit of your stories in this work.
— Teresa

CONTENTS

PREFACE

IT'S HARD TO WATCH THE NEWS TODAY without seeing the proliferation of politicians, athletes, and celebrities who are going through "rehab." Many are recognizing and acknowledging the brokenness of their lives and seeking the help they are unable to provide for themselves — or by themselves.

But where is the church in the world of recovery? How are God's people — and particularly those called to lead and shepherd — responding to this addiction crisis?

When I (Liz) applied for the position of Leadership Community Director at Leadership Network, a job that would include a focus on church recovery ministries, I went through a pretty typical interview process with the team that did the hiring. Then, just before the interview ended, I was asked a question that caught me off guard.

"Liz, have you ever dealt with an addiction yourself?"

Truth be told, no one had *ever* asked me that question before! I panicked. Suddenly my years of working in ministry, the Bible studies I'd led, the training I'd given on how to share the gospel — it all meant nothing. I hesitated to respond. There was a secret I had never shared with anyone.

"Yes, I have."

Though I had never told anyone, in my twenties I had struggled for several years with bulimia, an eating disorder. Over the years, I had kept it buried inside. It was too shameful to admit. After all, how could a Christian who was trying to trust God act out in this inappropriate way? I had accepted the idea that the church is no place for such a person. I was certain that if my secret was known, I would no longer fit in.

But I've learned that I'm not alone in feeling this way. Many Christians have issues, hurts, wounds, hidden sins, and addictions that they believe have no place in the church, and so they hide. They hide because they're convinced that they are the only ones struggling. They hide because they are ashamed and afraid to admit they need help.

According to research done by George Barna's organization, the number of Christians who struggle with addiction and brokenness is higher than we'd like to think. In every study, which includes thousands of interviews with born-again Christians, no clear evidence was shown that Christians are living transformed lives. In a study released in 2007, many of the lifestyle activities of born-again Christians were revealed to be statistically no different from others in the study. When asked to identify their activities over the last thirty days, born-again believers were just as likely to indicate that they had bet or gambled, visited a pornographic website, stolen something, consulted a medium or psychic, fought or abused someone, consumed enough alcohol to be considered legally drunk, used an illegal drug, lied, sought revenge, or said mean things about another person.[1]

I've found that recovery isn't just for those few people who really need help. It's something we all need at one point or another in our lives. Recovery is nothing more, but certainly nothing less, than the process of redeeming lives, learning to live in light of what Jesus has done for us. The reality of sin means that all of us are broken. All of us are flawed. All of us sin and are sinned against. All of us have been hurt and disappointed by others. Grief, wounds, death, and broken relationships tear at the fabric of our souls. We manage to survive, but we don't thrive. Our pain-management methods — alcohol, recreational drugs, pornography, sex, food, and, yes, even work — are temporary, fleeting, repetitive, and destructive. The unbroken pattern is the same in so many of our lives: pain, relief, shame, pain, relief, shame — spiraling ever downward. The velocity of the descent varies, but the direction is constant. We need a realistic understanding of how to work through our issues, our struggles with sinful behavior, so we can experience more than just relief from our struggles. We want to grow, but to really grow in faith, we need support and we need a safe place to find answers to our questions. We all need recovery in different ways, for different reasons, but we all want to see lives restored and healed by the grace of God.

In the meantime, with our untreated wounds and addictions, we fill the seats during weekend worship, sit on elders boards, serve as prayer warriors, and even stand in pulpits. We want to recover. We want to be restored. But sometimes it feels as if our desperate and sincere prayers go unanswered, and we are left wondering, "Why do the promises of peace, healing, and transformation seem to elude me and my family?"

When I began this journey of gathering churches to focus on the lack of effective solutions to this problem, I began a quest to learn what recovery is, what it looks like in the church, and whether it's a viable ministry. Are there churches where God is at work healing lives and restoring people to wholeness? I conducted thirty- to sixty-minute interviews with more than 260 churches around the United States and Canada, most of them large churches with a weekend worship-service attendance of more than fifteen hundred. I spoke with many lead pastors, but most often I talked with recovery pastors, recovery directors, care pastors, and church counselors — the people who have their fingers on the pulse of the emotional health of the church. I also interviewed some individuals who didn't work directly with the church but were Christian leaders in this field of recovery. I read scores of books on various recovery-related topics and attended numerous conferences over a period of several years.

In the midst of my research, I met Teresa McBean, the coauthor of this book. I knew from the beginning that we shared a similar passion for the church and the ministry of recovery. Teresa and her team have successfully planted three recovery communities — churches where people are experiencing the freedom that is found only in Christ. She possesses a depth of understanding about the day in and day out workings of recovery ministry in the church. Her practical working knowledge of the field along with my research and extensive exposure to recovery ministries across the nation have made collaborating on this project a natural fit.

There are many different approaches to recovery ministry in the church today. There is no "one size fits all" pattern for effective and transformative ministry. And the good news is that across the nation, hopeless and helpless people are finding their way back to God, both within the four walls of the church and outside our traditional structures, through the door of recovery. They are experiencing transformation. Their prayers for changed lives are being answered. They are finding church to be a place where they can tell the truth about their lives without fear, where they can experience the grace they've longed for but felt they didn't deserve. Some with addictions that have been labeled untreatable, who have been considered unredeemable, are now experiencing soul restoration. *By the blood of Christ*

This book tells the stories of those working in these ministries, people who believe in miracles because they witness them on a regular basis! Instead of simply highlighting one or two models for ministry, this book shows the remarkable diversity of church recovery models, making it a unique resource unlike any other work written on the subject of recovery.

Why the Church?

The nature and purpose of the church is to be a people in community who experience Jesus and live out what Jesus did while he was on earth. For this reason, the church is called "the body" of Christ. Jesus says in Luke 19:10, "The Son of Man came to seek and to save what was lost." Although Jesus certainly came to seek the lost — those far from God — his ministry was really about saving, restoring, and recovering *what* was lost at the fall. Everything that was lost to us in our sin and rebellion against God has been redeemed at the cross and will one day be completely restored. Until that time of final restoration, God invites his followers to join him in bringing that restoration to the lives of broken and hurting people.

Luke 9:11 reveals to us a little bit about how Jesus organized his gathering, his "church," if we can use that term. "He welcomed them and spoke to them about the kingdom of God, and healed those who needed healing." Jesus' church was a place where everyone felt welcome and wanted. They were part of a family. In speaking to them about the kingdom, Jesus was giving them a vision for how life would be different under the reign of God. His vision inspired hope. But he not only inspired hearts with his words; he healed those who needed healing.

We think this is a pretty good outline for what church should be — a place of radical hospitality, inexhaustible hope, and transformational healing, a place where we recover what was lost in the fall. A place where God is at work, changing lives, every day.

Bridges to God's Grace

There is a huge gap between where people are in their lives and where they desire to be. Even the most devout believers regularly find themselves in a place where God's restorative grace seems out of reach.

We may not be able to immediately change the way a person feels, but the church can begin by building a bridge that will connect the spiritually bereft to the throne of God's grace, a bridge for hurting people who believe that they have nowhere to go. A church that understands the power of grace and refrains from condemnation can, through a ministry of recovery, offer people the gift of hope and become a place where vision is renewed and people are healed. The church offers an atmosphere of acceptance and puts in place the unique elements necessary for the process of restoration to begin. The church of Jesus provides bridges to the grace we all long to experience.

We wrote this book with several groups in mind:

- Curious pastors who may not be ready to start a recovery ministry, yet want to hear about what other churches are doing to help meet needs in their congregations.
- Pastors and leaders who are ready to start a ministry of recovery and want to get a broad overview of how various churches have approached the ministry.
- Leaders who have tried to do recovery but have not seen the success they hoped for.
- Recovery leaders who may have experienced growth and health in their ministries but feel they are alone, perhaps even feel perplexed over why more churches aren't embracing recovery ministry.

We also tried to provide the answers to these questions:

- Why do churches start recovery ministries?

- How do we begin this type of ministry, and what are the options?
- What have other churches learned that might help us?

We hope that this book, through the medium of story, will not only inspire but also educate. You will learn that recovery is never easy, and it can even be quite messy! But more important, you will discover that there are simple things you can do that will help your church become the place you want it to be — a place of hope, healing, and transformation, a true bridge to grace. Our prayer is that when people who are hurting walk into your church, they will find their way to the throne of God's grace.

> We do not have a high priest who is unable to sympathize with our weaknesses, but we have one who has been tempted in every way, just as we are — yet was without sin. Let us then approach the throne of grace with confidence, so that we may receive mercy and find grace to help us in our time of need.
> — Hebrews 4:15 – 16

IN APPRECIATION

TOGETHER WE'D LIKE TO THANK KRISTA PETTY from Backyard Impact, who served as our editor, along with Ryan Pazdur, Chris Fann, Jane Haradine, Grace Olson, Brian Phipps, and the team at Zondervan for their thoroughness, attention to detail, and passion in giving editorial oversight to this project.

We give a special thanks to John Baker for his contribution to the ministry of recovery by establishing Celebrate Recovery at Saddleback Church in Lake Forest, California. In 1991, John had a vision to launch a Christ-centered approach to helping people with hurts, hang-ups, and destructive habits. Today more than ten thousand churches around the world have started Celebrate Recovery ministries, and more than five hundred thousand people have walked through the Celebrate Recovery process.

From Liz

I want to thank Tom Wilson of Leadership Network, who first had the vision for a Recovery Ministry Leadership Community. I am thankful for Bob Buford and my friends at Leadership Network for the wonderful opportunity they gave me to invest in this most important ministry.

I want to give a shout-out to each of the fifty-five church teams that convened in Dallas four times over two years as a part of the Recovery Ministry Leadership Community. Thank you for being my tutors along this journey.

Many thanks to Teresa McBean, my friend, mentor, and coauthor. I really couldn't have written this book without you.

To Dr. Bill Thrall for his insight, teaching, and contributions to the recovery teams and to my life, and to Dr. Dale Ryan, who has blazed the trail for this movement.

To Deb Haberer, Pat Runyon, Janet Hauser, Jan Horner, Diane Gorsuch, and Dr. Bryan Munroe, who walked me through my own recovery.

To Natalie Rice and Kacey Olson, who kindly listened and gave me input as I read them each chapter.

And a big thank-you and hug to my husband, Eric, whose love, encouragement, and confidence in me keep me going.

From Teresa

In 1999, I didn't know a single thing about recovery, other than the fact that all of us need it and many of us don't know it. Along the way, so many people have given so much to make it possible for me to participate in a recovery ministry.

My husband, Pete, and I have some amazing friends who have supported us in more ways than we can acknowledge in this grand, epic adventure. Thank you, one and all.

Our NorthStar Community family continues to encourage, guide, and direct me so I can learn from them. Our NorthStar staff and volunteers have carried an extra load while I've been holed up in my office writing. I want to express my gratitude for the privilege of working alongside each of you and for your willingness to share in the bearing of burdens each and every day.

Bon Air Baptist Church did the unimaginable by entrusting a group of lay leaders with this new thing. Without this first step, I certainly wouldn't have explored the concept of faith-based recovery, much less found my calling.

A few years ago Leadership Network and its team of contributors brought together groups of recovery ministries. We were privileged to be part of that process. Their efforts to support and encourage recovery ministries around the nation have forever changed the face of faith-based recovery. Recovery can be an isolating ministry. Leadership Network gave us all a chance to connect, collaborate, and expand our perspectives. They brought in speakers like Dale Ryan, Don Simmons, Archibald Hart, and Bill Thrall, who blessed us with their expertise and the transfer of their knowledge, but more than anything, these giants among mere mortals offered practitioners a safe place to go for support when we needed a helping hand.

Liz Swanson put us all together, and I particularly want to thank her for bringing the various communities together in such a Spirit-filled manner. At many points along the way, she became the glue that held us together.

Once Liz and I started writing, a host of people read and critiqued, corrected, and corralled our efforts. We can't thank you enough for the gentleness with which you provided feedback.

Our editing team, Zondervan, and the churches that allowed us to share their stories spent enormous amounts of time and energy helping us craft this work.

No acknowledgment would be complete without expressing appreciation to my husband, Pete, and our three children. More than twenty years ago Pete made a difficult career decision so I could go to school one evening a week without feeling an ounce of anxiety about our children's care and feeding. We didn't know how each step of faith would lead to another, but we walked it together, and I thank Pete, Meredith, Scott, and Michael for the joy they bring to the journey. (Most of all, I thank them for their wise decision to institute the "don't ask, don't tell" policy regarding what went on at home when I was away!)

To the extent that I contributed anything to this book, I hope and pray that it is as a messenger of hope on behalf of all the people who have shown me what it means to trust God by living with nothing hidden and, in so doing, learning how to live a righteous life by loving others well. You inspire me.

INTRODUCTION
The Tattoos Tell the Story

I prayed to be spared another day of guilt and depression and addiction.

— *Josh Hamilton, outfielder, Texas Rangers*

IT WAS JULY OF 2008 AT THE HOME RUN DERBY, and Josh Hamilton of the Texas Rangers was the last one up for the day. The young batter stood at the plate, and as pitch after pitch came at him, he swung at each one, hitting them all. One, then two, then three, then four home runs in a row. But it didn't stop there. He continued to smack pitches out of the ballpark an additional twenty-four times, ending with a record-breaking twenty-eight homers. The crowd went wild! It was an incredible moment to witness, a thing of beauty.

As thrilling as Hamilton's performance at the Home Run Derby was, there is an even bigger story to tell about his life, the story that made his spectacular performance even possible. Hamilton's story was later featured in *Sports Illustrated*. And the lead-in to the article contained a surprising twist: "After drugs and alcohol nearly destroyed his career before it got started, a repentant Josh Hamilton has miraculously restored the skills that now make him a Triple Crown threat."[2] In 2010, Hamilton was voted MVP of the American League and was selected by his peers as *Sporting News* magazine's player of the year.[3]

Josh still bears the menacing and telling tattoos that were inked from his neck to his hands in the darker periods of his life. During a time when he was deeply addicted to drugs, he accumulated twenty-six tattooed images on his body, a few of which were described in the article: "Satan's face gazes out from the crook of his left elbow, blue flames shoot down both his forearms; he now regrets getting every one of them."[4]

After years of heading in and out of rehab, Josh finally began taking steps toward true and lasting recovery. Following an encounter with God, he began to experience some healing and tried to remove some of the more daunting tattoos, which no longer symbolized his life. But he quickly realized that the process was too painful. Those tattoos, so difficult to remove, now serve as a reminder of where he has come from, and of the bridge he crossed to discover the grace and mercy that helped him in his time of desperate need. The tattoos now tell his story. How, exactly, did his life change so radically?

Josh's story makes sense only when we define and understand what the ministry of recovery is all about. So what is recovery? A good place to start is to describe what recovery is not:

- It is not merely a twelve-step program for alcoholics and those other people who have *real* problems.

- It is not simply support groups for those who can't seem to trust God like the rest of us do.

- It is not a place to send people when you just don't know what else to do with them.

- It is not a revival where the crowd is whipped into a frenzy, to the point where everyone shares their greatest secret sin.

Recovery is a process that often begins in a place of desperation. In Josh's case, he lost everything and hit rock bottom. Only then did he finally surrender his life to God — the first step toward recovery. Josh began to work his way, one day at a time, back from the depths of his addiction. His life was no longer controlled by his addiction, but his addiction still defined (and defines to this day) certain aspects of his life. He knows what he *must* avoid so as not to fall back into a lifestyle of drug use. Part of Josh's recovery has involved sharing his secret sin with the world, making his struggle public.

There are many stories about people who have been redeemed by God and transformed in miraculous ways. These changed lives are a tribute to the goodness of God and his healing grace and to the faithful people who were willing to help those who struggle.

But for every story of triumph, there are scores of other stories of people who are still struggling with secret fears, anxieties, phobias, wounds, depressions, addictions, and sexual struggles. Who are these people, and why do they continue to struggle? Are they the people on the fringe, seldom attending church services, living their lives in the world in open rebellion toward God? Or are they people close to us, with secrets hidden so well that we don't even recognize them? You may be surprised to learn that those who struggle are not only among us; sometimes they are the ones who lead us:

- He got a call from his son. "Dad, I am in jail. I need help. I can't stop drinking." (Pastors a church of three thousand.)

- He thought after the affair that God would never be able to use him again. (Pastors a church of twenty-five hundred.)

- She held a full-time position teaching at a seminary, but she was an alcoholic. (Pastors a church of thirty-five hundred.)

- His son is in jail for dealing drugs. (Pastors a church of five hundred in a city of fifteen hundred.)

- A successful pastor, writer, and keynote Christian speaker at the national level, he had his secret affair disclosed. (No longer a pastor.)

- A gay masseuse revealed this pastor's secret life to the world during a TV interview. (In process of restoration.)

- He was hooked on prescription drugs and was a functioning alcoholic. He lost his family, his position, and his dignity as he stood before the board of his denomination and was "defrocked." (Pastors in a recovery ministry.)

- He fell into a deep depression that he could not shake and was hospitalized twice. (Pastors a church of four thousand.)

- He was arrested in a sting operation when he attempted to meet with a thirteen-year-old girl he had "courted" online. (Relieved of his position as associate pastor of a church of ten thousand.)

- Pornography so gripped him, he had to leave the mission field. (He was restored through recovery and is again in ministry.)

- One of his sons left home and lived in complete rebellion to everything his dad stood for. One of his daughters married and divorced. His granddaughter got pregnant at sixteen and was estranged from her grandparents and parents. (The most famous evangelist of our time, Billy Graham.)

Pastors and church leaders are not immune from the lure of temptation and the struggle with addiction, and in fact there is a long history of biblical heroes who struggled with patterns of sin.

What Is Recovery?

Many of our biblical heroes experienced their own desperate need for recovery. Godly men and women had affairs, committed murder, abused their power, got drunk, argued with their ministry partners, abandoned Jesus, and deserted their posts. They got depressed and discouraged. They became fearful and lost their nerve. But woven throughout these tales is evidence of God's redeeming of the lost.

God continues to redeem the lost today. The essence of recovery, for the purpose of this book, is focusing on the reality that the Christian life seldom matches the image many of us have created in our minds. When we look around, life may seem to be going beautifully. But what often is hidden, even in our own lives, is the brokenness and hurt we all experience. Recovery is at the heart of everything Jesus came to do. It's at the heart of the gospel. It's not a stretch to say that Jesus' first public sermon, recorded in Luke 4:18 – 19, was on the topic of recovery.

Recovery begins with the freedom to tell the truth about our lives, the real truth, in a safe place with appropriate people in the body of Christ. God can meet us only where we are, not where we wish we were or pretend we are. Recovery ministry is not a new ministry model but rather an attempt to replicate the ministry Jesus was focused on. He came to seek and save that which was lost (Luke

19:10). Recovery ministry helps many who have lost their way. It forms a bridge to a place they can't seem to find on their own.

We like how the authors of *The Journey of Recovery* Bible explain the process of recovery: "Recovery includes being honest about the past hurts so they can be healed, gaining insights about destructive patterns of behavior so they can be changed, developing trust in God as the source of wisdom and strength, and finding hope to replace shame and despair. Through this process a person can be recreated to live the way God intended."[5]

Churches approach recovery in different ways, but two core values drive every church-based recovery ministry:

1. The message that Christ's redemptive power is complete.
2. The reality that humans struggle daily in trying to live out this truth.

We believe that the power of the gospel is complete and sufficient to bring God's healing to those struggling with addictions and brokenness. But we also recognize that this healing isn't always immediate. In fact, it is often a daily struggle to appropriate God's grace as we live out the truth of what Christ has done for us.

And lest we think this is a ministry for those who are far from Christ or for those who are new in their faith, we need to recognize an important truth about the church today. Those within the walls of our churches struggle with the exact same issues as do those outside our church walls. The same sinful patterns, temptations, and addictive habits that afflict unbelievers also keep followers of Christ in bondage.

I know this is true, because it was true in my own life.

Broken by Addiction

As I mentioned earlier, I (Liz) faced my own struggle with addiction in my midtwenties, a struggle with an eating disorder known as bulimia. But the struggle with bulimia was simply the fruit of an ongoing struggle with something deeper, a struggle with loss.

When I was six years old, my mother was diagnosed with cancer, and after five years of treatments and hospitalizations, she died. As a young girl, suddenly without a mother, I did the best I could. I moved on with my life and tried to cope with the loss, but at eleven years old, I had very little understanding of how to cope. I stuffed my emotions deep inside my heart and tried to act normal. I tried to be like the other kids I saw around me, kids who had mothers.

Despite my efforts at hiding my pain, I failed. Problems began to develop, and by the time I was seventeen, I started suffering from unexplained fears. To alleviate my fears, I would walk into the house at night and turn on every light. Since we had a large house and I lived on one side while the rest of the family lived on the other, no one noticed.

During my senior year in high school, a friend invited me to a concert at her church. As the group sang and talked, I recognized a quality of life I had not seen before in my casual brush with Christianity. Deep inside, I realized that I wanted what they had, something I had been missing. So when the opportunity to receive Christ was given, I stepped forward. I believed the invitation. I believed God's Word was true. I believed Jesus had answers for me. I just didn't know how they would work in my daily struggles. Although I had made a sincere commitment to Christ, there was something within me that still needed healing. I had faith but no direction concerning how to deal with the loss I had suffered.

After entering college, I began a ritual that I later learned had its own name — bulimia. Every day, I would secretly steal away and eat until I was almost sick. Then I would sneak off to the bathroom and purge — a delicate way of saying that I threw my guts up. I continued this secret ritual off and on for years, even after going into full-time ministry. I was trapped, a slave to my bulimia.

Then one day, a young girl in one of my Bible studies took me aside and shared with me that she had a problem. She didn't know who to talk to. She told me she would eat until she almost felt sick, and then she would throw up.

I was stunned. Speechless. She had described exactly what I was doing, but I had never admitted it to anyone. I felt so ashamed, and I had no words to comfort her. I knew that I wasn't ready to share my own struggles with her. Looking back, I'm sure that young girl felt even more guilt and shame after her confession to me.

In fact, I still cringe when I think about that moment. This young woman had come to me in her weakness, asking for help, and I shrugged her off. Her questions had triggered my own unresolved issues and left me ashamed and afraid. An accusing voice in my head was shouting at me, "And who are *you* to try to help her? Who are you trying to kid?"

But that experience, shameful as it was, prepared me for that critical moment at the end of my interview for the position of Leadership Director of Recovery Ministries at Leadership Network. At that interview — for the first time in my life — I was finally able to tell the truth, that I had struggled for years with a serious, shameful addiction.

The Wisdom of Experience

After I was hired by Leadership Network to lead the charge for recovery ministry, I began meeting with several experts on the issue. And one of the first people I talked to was Dr. Dale Ryan, who teaches recovery at Fuller Theological Seminary and is the founder of the National Association for Christian Recovery (NACR) and Christian Recovery International. He understands the desperate needs we see in the church today and is working to help the church fulfill its mission to offer grace to the wounded and hurting.

"Recovery is the process of healing and growth," Dr. Ryan writes in his book *Rooted in God's Love*. "[It] is not a set of new insights into the human condition. Recovery goes back as far as human history. God has always been in the business of bringing change, growth and healing to people who are struggling with the most difficult of life's experiences."[6]

Churches that focus on the ministry of recovery find ways to help the brokenhearted know that God does indeed know their weaknesses and is both capable and willing to restore them to health and wholeness. As I have traveled around the United States and Canada, interviewing the leaders of more than 260 churches about the specific things they are doing to help people overcome addictions and problems in their lives, one of the questions I have always asked is, "What are some of the greatest challenges you face as you attempt to develop a ministry of recovery?" The answer usually includes some variation on these two responses:

- Making the church a safe place where people can tell the truth about their struggles without being labeled, judged, and condemned.
- Creating an authentic place where people find others who are willing to tell the truth about their own issues, a place where there are no masks.

Our hope is that this book will guide you as you seek to answer this question for your church or ministry. In these pages, you'll find stories of how churches are learning to create an environment where safety and authenticity breed repentance, ultimately leading to lasting transformation.

Many of our churches are filled with people who have secret sins and struggles. Recovery ministries help people bring those secrets out from the darkness and into the light, into the loving embrace of God's grace. Josh Hamilton publicly struggled for years, living in bondage to his addictions and sins, afraid to set foot in a church. My struggle with bulimia, on the other hand, was a story that remained hidden for many years. Though I lacked the visible tattoos that Josh has on his body, I had hidden scars on my heart. For years, I showed up in my regular seat at church, carefully hiding my scars, afraid to share my struggles.

Today the church is changing. Recovery ministries around North America are giving people permission to talk about their struggles and providing safe places for them heal. Join us as we discover the amazing things God is doing and find innovative approaches to recovery ministry, approaches that can transform your church community from a place of fear and shame to a life-giving ministry of grace and healing.

Questions for Reflection and Discussion

1. What comes to your mind when you think of the phrase *recovery ministry*? What has been your experience with recovery ministry in the past?

2. Have you ever found yourself in a place of desperation? If so, describe how you felt.

3. Rank your church on whether it is a safe place where people find freedom to tell the truth about their lives. Use a scale of one to ten, with one being not safe at all and ten being very safe.

4. Where is your safe place?

5. Which of these words best describe the current ministries of your church: welcoming, healing, restoring, honest?

chapter one

IT ALL BEGINS WITH YOU

Christian Assemblies Church

> I became more desperate to follow Christ than to pastor a
> church, so I began to preach from my own broken life as I
> taught the Scriptures.... I had learned to do church but had
> forgotten how to do Christ.
>
> — *Pastor Mark Pickerel*

WHEN YOU LOOK AT IT FROM THE OUTSIDE, the church
building that houses the congregation of Christian Assemblies
Church in Eagle Rock, California, is really nothing to brag about,
but as I (Liz) entered the sanctuary that morning for worship, it
was packed out. Those in the gathered body, standing and sitting, reflected the surrounding neighborhood in age and ethnicity.
Located on the edge of downtown Los Angeles, this is a church filled
with Hispanics, African Americans, Asians, Middle Easterners,
Pacific Islanders, and Caucasians. Christian Assemblies isn't your
typical, homogeneous church, yet it is growing and thriving as a mul-
tiethnic community of faith.

I had been traveling around the United States and Canada for
almost three years at this point, visiting churches and sitting in services, and yet when I arrived at Christian Assemblies in Los Angeles,
something struck me as different. "They get it," I thought. "They
really get it!" I knew very little about the church apart from what my

niece, Sunny, had told me when she invited me. "All I can tell you is that this church understands recovery," she had said.

She was right.

Authenticity and Grace

As we worshiped together that morning, it was almost as if you could sense the presence of God in the atmosphere of authenticity and grace. After the service, I found some time to meet with Mark Pickerel, the senior pastor of Christian Assemblies, and listen to him as he shared the story of the church and how God was working to bring freedom to people's lives.

It all started about twenty years ago when the church was going through a very difficult transition. Much of the church's structure was being changed at that time, and the entire congregation was going through a time of "great searching." Mark said that he too had been trying to figure out what was going on in his life. "I had learned to do church but had forgotten how to do Christ." About this time, he became fascinated by a group of alcoholics who began attending the church. "They wouldn't compromise at any point. They were so honest, even ruthlessly so, about their own lives and failures." Mark later found out that these men were faithful members and regular attenders of Alcoholics Anonymous (AA).

At the time, Mark was also meeting regularly with Dr. Archibald Hart, a renowned psychologist and Christian leader who was teaching at Fuller Seminary. He had been helping Mark work through the issues that had caused such chaos in his church. Mark explained to Dr. Hart his fascination with this group whose members were so honest and devoted to AA. Dr. Hart suggested that he attend a meeting to see what he might discover.

So one Thursday night, Mark drove out to the San Fernando Valley to attend his first AA meeting. As he walked into the room, he began to realize that he was truly anonymous. Nobody there knew he was a pastor. Nor did they care. "They assumed I was just another drunk who needed to get sober, and they embraced me with a grace that was truly overwhelming." One of the guys, who didn't look as if he could rub two nickels together, even came up and offered to buy Mark a "Big Book" (the book *Alcoholics Anonymous*, which is the framework of AA, including the Twelve Steps to recovery). Mark thanked the man for his kind offer, amazed that a man with far fewer resources than Mark had was willing to buy a book for a complete stranger. Mark decided to buy the book himself, and he sat down to see how the rest of the meeting unfolded.

Everything that happened was very new for Mark. He didn't know the rules, and he felt out of place when everyone stood up and repeated a mantra declaring that they were a mess and needed help. Then, when everyone sat down, a nicely dressed, successful-looking businessman went to the podium. He began to talk about how his week was going, and at one point he became very quiet and said, "I felt so pressed ... but I didn't drink." The group began to clap and cheer as they shared in his victory. He then received a "ninety-day chip," indicating that he had gone almost three months without a single drink.

After he sat down, a woman stood up to speak to the group. She too was nicely dressed and quite articulate, but Mark could tell as soon as she began to speak that her story was headed in a completely different direction. As she reflected on the ups and downs of her week, she ended by confessing her failure to the group: "But damn it, I drank this week," she said. Unlike her predecessor, she had relapsed into her old ways of coping.

Mark wasn't sure what would happen next. After all, the woman had failed. Would they yank her off the stage or boo her for her mistake? Much to his surprise, the crowd again stood up and applauded. The small group of people there surrounded her with love and encouragement. Why? Well, simply because she had shown up that night; it didn't matter that she had failed. She was there and she had shared her struggle. "I almost didn't know what to do with it," Mark said to me.

After the meeting was over, Mark walked to the parking lot and got into his car. It was raining hard that night, but he didn't drive home. In fact, he didn't even start the engine. "I just sat in my car and wept. There was something in me that ached to be a part of a group where it was okay to fail and, in the midst of failure, to know there was still a power that gives you a second chance, a new beginning, one that gives you the possibility of a fresh start."

That night, Mark Pickerel, a pastor, left an AA meeting having witnessed the power of a different kind of confession. While one of the people in the group had acknowledged his struggle and was able to celebrate his victory, another member of the group had admitted her failure. Both confessions of faith were celebrated. And in that anonymous meeting room — where there had been no mention of God or Jesus Christ — Mark Pickerel had seen a model of how to respond to hurting people. What he witnessed that night brought him to tears. Why? Because Mark knew that the power of confession and repentance, so vital to spiritual growth and transformation, wasn't present in his church.

Replicating the Meeting

Mark reported back to Dr. Hart on his experience at the AA meeting, acknowledging his concerns about his church: "I thought that to be successful, I had to be better, bigger, and faster. But at that meeting, people embraced me with a kind of grace that was really overwhelming." Mark decided to do something about it. He sensed that God was calling him to create a place that was characterized by grace and acceptance in action, a church where God's love could be seen and felt by anyone who attended. "If somebody comes to church that week and has succeeded, we'll stand and applaud the grace of God that gave him the power to do what brought him success. But if someone fails, we will also stand and applaud him because there is still the hope of grace that can change him."

Attending the AA meeting gave a new focus to Mark's life. As he returned to the pulpit the next week, he began to make some practical changes in the way he was leading the church. "I realized that even though I was not an alcoholic, I too was desperate. I was a man who was hiding from others." Mark didn't have a grand plan or a new strategy, but as he describes it, "I became more desperate to follow Christ than to pastor a church, and I began to preach from my own broken life as I taught the Scriptures." Mark found himself revealing more of his own struggles to the church. As he shared honestly on Sunday mornings, he found not only that he was experiencing the power of healing but also that his vulnerability in the pulpit was beginning to change the culture of the church. "People were saying to me, 'This is what it looks like to follow Jesus. This is what it means to confess our sins one to another.'" As Mark confessed and shared his struggle with sin, he wasn't just giving out a laundry list of his personal shortcomings. He began to speak openly about his brokenness, his pain, his fears, and his failures. Because he spoke honestly, people connected with him, seeing him not as an aloof pastor but as a man who shared many of the same experiences they had.

Starting a Recovery Ministry

When Jim Cosby, the care pastor at Christian Assemblies, came to the church to start an "official" recovery ministry, he simply built on the groundwork Mark had already laid. "The church had already become a church of grace," Jim said. "It was a place where people were welcomed and accepted just as they are. It was a place where no one needed to perform to be accepted. Christian Assemblies is the first place I found grace. I was a pastor who had utterly failed in the past. People I led did not get better; they got worse. And I didn't get better either. It wasn't that the gospel was broken—I was."

Jim told me that when he shifted from telling people what he thought they ought to know to telling them about his own brokenness and healing through Jesus, the people he was leading began to experience God's healing as well. All Jim had to do was provide a safe place for people to speak about their struggles, knowing they would receive help and not judgment or condemnation. "We aren't just about drugs, alcohol, and addictions; we're about helping broken people," he said.

Today Christian Assemblies exudes an atmosphere of grace. The way people express their faith is authentic and honest. People speak openly of their shortcomings, their setbacks, and the broken areas of their lives as well as of the power of God to heal and change. It's a church where everyone, including the pastoral staff, is in a process of recovery. No one pretends they have arrived. People experience the freedom to be exactly where they are in their spiritual journeys, and they are applauded simply for showing up.

We can learn several key lessons from Christian Assemblies' story, principles that help churches to successfully create a culture of acceptance and grace.

(1) *Recovery begins in the pulpit, not in the pews.* As a pastor, Mark understands the unique power that pastors have when they are honest and model what it means to have a growing relationship with Christ. Whenever he talks with church leaders, he advises them to talk about their own journeys of faith, both the successes and the failures. "Don't always tell details," he says, "but be honest. If it has been a good week, talk about that. But if it hasn't been so good, talk about that too. This opens the door for others to feel the freedom to walk in the same way. There is a great need for transparency from anyone who is up front, not in the telling of coarse details for some kind of dramatic effect but in sharing honest struggles in a true spirit of authenticity and humility."

Admittedly, Mark's suggestion that pastors talk about their own sins and weaknesses runs counter to what most congregations expect from their leaders (and what leaders require of themselves). Pastors desire to practice what they preach; congregants rightfully hope their leaders lead with integrity. To be candid, these expectations are onerous and seductive, creating an environment that may hinder, rather than foster, recovery. While Mark's suggestion may seem naive, even risky, to many pastors, pew sitters and former church attenders report a longing for authenticity from the pulpit more than for an appearance of moral perfection. Mark does not suggest that pastors use the Sunday morning message as a personal therapy session. But he also warns that pastors who consistently fail to personalize their messages run into certain dangers. Listeners today may feel that the message is condescending or even just plain irrelevant to their lives, lives that are often filled with ongoing struggles against sin and brokenness.

Applying this lesson in a church setting requires care and sensitivity, but the failure to value honesty is a costly mistake. Honesty from the pulpit, properly communicated, can create a church culture that is conducive to helping people heal and experience intimacy with God and others.

(2) *Recovery in the church is possible when ministry leaders are willing to live with appropriate honesty and healthy self-disclosure.* The AA meeting that Mark attended was a vivid illustration to him of the words found in James 5:15 – 16: "If he has sinned, he will be forgiven. Therefore confess your sins to each other and pray for each other so that you may be healed." While it's true that corporate prayer was lacking in the AA meeting that night, confession of sin was embraced and was handled with more grace than Mark witnessed in his church.

In many ways, the very act of walking into an AA meeting room is a form of confession. These meetings are designed for people who are in trouble, people who need help, who have reached the end of their strength and want to change. No one sugarcoats the dire circumstances that AA members face. When a person steps through that door, every moment is dedicated to the very real act of confession. AA places a high value on creating an environment where it is safe for all attenders to honestly disclose their struggles without fear of reprisal or condemnation.

Isn't this what the church is supposed to be like?

Shouldn't the act of walking into a church be an act of confession, an acknowledgment that we're here because we need help? It's interesting to note that the word *confess* in Greek is *ekzomologeo*, which simply means "to declare or say out loud." Although many of us have grown accustomed to thinking of this word strictly in the sense of confessing our sins, that's not exactly what the text says. The word translated as "sins" in James 5:15 – 16 is the Greek word *paraptoma,* which describes a slip in some area of life. It refers to a person who has "fallen, failed, erred, or made some kind of mistake; a person who has accidentally bumped into something, accidentally swerved or turned amiss."[7]

Recovery begins with a public acknowledgment of a need for restoration, and it continues with a process for honest self-appraisal and the willingness to share that with others. Pastor Mark Pickerel became a broken healer when he recognized that he had veered from the road he had started on and had substituted the function of doing church for the freedom of experiencing Christ. It was his willingness to face his failure and talk about it that set the stage for a thriving recovery ministry at his church.

3. *Recovery is not about "sin management."* Christian Assemblies has created a grace-filled environment in their community of faith. When hurting people attend AA meetings or show up at a church, they are looking for something that will help them make their lives work. Bill Thrall, coauthor of *TrueFaced*, makes an important observation in his book. He talks about the attempt to handle sin outside of an environment of grace as "sin management." But sin cannot truly be managed. Bill writes, "Grace teaches us that God — and only God — can handle my sin."[8] According to Bill, "A sin-management system shuts off the only resource that can deal with sin: Our trust in whom God says we are and the power of his grace.... We cannot mature without the healing gifts of grace."[9] Sin management looks for a program, a plan, a methodology, and the willpower to do right and please God. When we understand that sin cannot be managed, we become willing to wrestle with what it means simply to trust God with the truth about who we are and what we do.

Grace-filled churches are the key to ending the all too common practice of sin management. The suggestion that churches get back into the business of dispensing grace has been ignored as a concept too obvious to merit serious consideration. Some have sharply criticized the concept, suggesting that perhaps these communities are soft on sin. But anyone who has attended an AA meeting knows that this is an unfair assessment. Recovering addicts understand that they are powerless over their affliction and that only God can save them. They know from experience that addiction cannot be managed. And they know that unless a solution is found, the inevitable result will be death. Addicts are serious about seeking freedom from addiction, and AA teaches that trusting in a power greater than ourselves is the only way out. Mark saw these principles lived out in the AA meeting he attended, and it radically changed his view of how the church could respond to sin.

4. *Recovery takes courage.* Mark's visit to AA exposed him to a community founded on the principles espoused in the Twelve Steps. (For a detailed description of the Twelve Steps and a model of how they can be adapted for use in many faith-based recovery ministries, see appendix A.) The Twelve Steps provide the structure, language, philosophy, and process that drive recovery ministry.

One of the key components of any twelve-step program is step four, which asks the participant to make a "searching and fearless moral inventory." This inventory requires each person to take a hard look at himself or herself, writing out a detailed account of both the positives and negatives of his or her personal moral history. This information provides the participant with a jumping-off point in the process of forgiveness and making amends that is essential for recovery. Taking an honest moral inventory is not easy. It often brings into the light issues and problems that have been hidden in darkness for years, sometimes decades. Courage, in this case, is doing what you know you ought to do.   ⤷ + Humility

Mark's exposure to AA left him open to change, but the actual process of change came about as he faced his failures and confessed them. Developing a successful ministry of recovery takes more than good intentions; it requires a determined commitment to face fears, and it requires the courage to address hard realities in our lives and in the lives of other people. Change is never easy.

5. *The environment we create matters more than the programs we offer.* Mark's vulnerability did more than inspire a response from the congregation; it sparked the creation of an entirely new culture of authenticity. Experiencing grace in action requires us to plan strategically for what we preach, what we teach, and how we organize ourselves as a church body. Recovery is more than adding a program or a class dealing with addictions or loss. We must work to create an environment, much like the one Mark witnessed at AA, where people model and demonstrate God's grace in their words and actions. Hurting people wander into churches in search of hope and healing. Before they ever get connected to a program or attend a class, they will sense the atmosphere of the church.

A few years ago, when a nationally known megachurch pastor confessed to his congregation his homosexual affairs, Dale Ryan, associate professor of recovery ministry at Fuller Theological Seminary, astutely observed that church elders also needed to focus on what was happening in the larger congregation. "There are at least a hundred people there who are struggling with homosexuality," he said, "but they are afraid to admit it. They are watching to see what the church does. The question is not just about [this pastor] but about how we become the kind of congregation where people can find help."

When the Pharisees dragged the woman caught in adultery to Jesus (John 8:3 – 11), onlookers gawked at the spectacle in much the same way we respond with morbid fascination when media outlets report modern-day scandalous behavior. What were they thinking? Did they stand shoulder-to-shoulder, jostling for a better view while feeling alone with their secret sins and fear of public exposure? Did anyone in the crowd have the wherewithal to wonder, "What if I were the one standing before Jesus and my community with all my secrets exposed? How would I be treated?"

People continue to watch and wonder how communities of faith will respond to the confession of sin and shortcomings. Who among us hasn't had the fleeting, anxious thought, "What would happen if all my secret sins were publicly exposed?"

Grace applauds those who succeed, but it also claps for those who just keep showing up week after week.

Questions for Reflection and Discussion

1. How comfortable are you with listening to people confess their sins? Explain.

2. When do people in your church applaud others? Who is given status in your church — those who look like they have it all together, or those who are willing to wrestle with their issues?

3. Where are you seeing signs of people getting better?

4. Are some in your church getting worse? If so, in what way?

5. Does the environment in your church encourage people to just show up? If not, explain.

chapter two

WHAT THE MRI REVEALED
Woodcrest Chapel

> We invite people to embrace their brokenness. This has some benefits and some risks, but we cannot escape it. It is our calling. We're real people on a real journey.
> — *Pastor Pieter Van Waarde*

I (LIZ) STILL FEEL A BIT EMBARRASSED when I remember my first meeting with the staff at Woodcrest Chapel in Columbia, Missouri. At the time, I was working with Leadership Network and was helping staff a Leadership Network multisite church conference in Southern California. We were asked to make connections with the leadership of various churches attending the conference, and so I called Pieter Van Waarde, introduced myself, and invited him and his staff to join me for lunch. We gathered around the table at a local restaurant, and I began to ask questions about the church and its history. Piet talked about his initial days with the church and explained the difficulty he had making the transition into leadership at a church where their previous pastor had had to resign because of a moral failure. I had just learned from someone that when a pastor suffers a moral failure, there is about a 70 percent chance that the next pastor the church hires will do the same thing, because churches tend to be attracted to a certain personality type and leadership style. Without thinking through the implications, I helpfully communicated that information to the entire table. Understandably, there was an awkward silence after my remarks. Then Piet smiled at me and said, "Well, I sure hope that's not gonna be true about me!"

Assuming the role of senior pastor following the departure of the founding pastor of a church can be quite a challenge. Transitions like these are filled with the inevitable comparisons, the changing of the culture, and the introduction of new methods and styles of leadership. But when Pieter Van Waarde began to assume his new leadership position at Woodcrest Chapel, he noticed that something was happening, something odd. Although everything was moving along smoothly — by all outward appearances — Piet observed that there were several unresolved issues lingering beneath the surface: issues of pain, hurt, betrayal, and mistrust. Some dysfunctional behavior had emerged during several board and staff leadership meetings. On a regular and recurring basis, it felt as if the molehills of ministry were turning into mountains. Little disagreements between people would quickly escalate into major confrontations. The energy and the emotion people felt when they shared their frustration seemed to far exceed what was merited. "It felt completely out of sorts," Piet said.

And he was right. Something was definitely wrong.

Woodcrest Chapel is a multisite church located in Columbia, Missouri, a city of ninety-five thousand that sits in the center of the state. The church was started in 1987 with seven people meeting in the home of the founding pastor. Within two years, the church's attendance grew to more than one hundred people, and it continued to climb each year. From the pastor's living room, they transitioned into rented space at a Holiday Inn and eventually to an auditorium of their own. Woodcrest Chapel experienced great success and rapid growth.

But after several years, the founding pastor began having some serious emotional issues that ultimately led him to a breakdown and resulted in the public confession of some deep moral failures. When his sin was revealed, the congregation felt betrayed and bewildered. Their loss and disappointment left them in a state of grief, and it was the ongoing grief that was expressing itself now, often in very unhealthy ways.

Problems of the Past

As Piet observed the communication problems, habits of overreacting, and high levels of emotion over small disagreements, he began to recognize what was happening. The outward signs seemed similar to the behavior of individuals who bury their pain and stifle their emotions after difficult and troubling emotional experiences. When sufficient time and opportunity to heal are not given to people after a traumatic experience, they often seek an outlet for their pain and frustration. Sometimes that outlet can lead to inappropriate, unhealthy behavior, and Piet knew from personal experience the kind of destruction that can result from unstated and unresolved emotional conflict. He considered how he could best respond, and he decided to address the entire church in a series of sermons called Getting Past Your Past.

In his sermon series, Piet started out by sharing his own past, his own story. He felt that the best way to introduce the topic of honesty, anger, and hurt was to first unveil his own troubled past. This was a risky decision. In fact, his new associate pastor, Rod Casey, tried to talk him out of it, warning him of the potential fallout, particularly with the church in such a vulnerable emotional state.

But Piet was convinced it would work to simply be honest about his own struggles. "You can't survive in life without appropriately dealing with your emotions." Piet felt that if the church was ever going to experience genuine change and growth, the members needed to address how their past, which had been shrouded in guilt, shame, pain, and unforgiveness, was preventing them from experiencing the power of God's transforming grace.

Piet's Story

Most of us don't just end up somewhere. Little decisions are made, a compromise here, a compromise there, and the ruts get a little deeper and the path is set. Piet and his family moved from the Netherlands to New York City in 1957, when he was three years old. Piet struggled to fit in. Although he came from a strong Christian family, his family's church was old world and traditional, seemingly oblivious to the challenges of the twentieth century. In an attempt to find his place in high school, Piet began making a series of bad choices, little compromises that turned into a lifestyle, the details of which he shared with his congregation in the controversial sermon series Getting Past Your Past. He shared with the congregation a moment of clarity that he experienced during a particularly hard night of partying:

> The stench of spilled bong juice filled the air. Half-empty beer cans were leaking around the trash can in the corner of my one-bedroom apartment. I had partaken in some strange mixture of microdot, hash, and beer. It was 2:00 a.m. and I was sitting on a ragged couch with my best friend, Chuck, surveying the mess.
>
> Apparently people had fun; the trashed apartment was evidence of that. I don't remember much of the evening myself. It hurt to think.
>
> In the midst of my stupor, Chuck said, "Hey, Piet, we are always going to live like this!" He was excited about that prospect. For the first time in years, I was not. Chuck's words haunted me, "We're always going to live like this."
>
> In the weeks leading up to the party, I had witnessed firsthand the real life consequences of the so-called party life. Good friends were getting addicted to cocaine and stealing money to support their habit. Dealer friends were going to prison. I really didn't want to live like this anymore.
>
> How do good people end up in places like this?[10]

At about the same time, Piet's mother, Kitty, became deeply depressed and was hospitalized in a psych ward. She began going through a series of dramatic therapy techniques. The crisis further intensified when her youngest child, only two weeks old, died. Piet's mother simply could not recover from the loss. It was during this time, in the midst of death and depression, that Piet first learned about the source of his mother's depression, a family secret that had been hidden for years.

Secrets Revealed

Piet learned that his grandparents had been missionaries in Indonesia during World War II. When the Japanese invaded Indonesia, all of the Dutch, including Piet's grandparents and his mother, had been moved to prison camps. There they were beaten and tortured for almost four years. At the time, his mother was only six years old. Some of her formative years as a child had been spent in this environment, and the experience was so traumatic for the family that they made a pact never to speak of it again.

And they never did.

Unfortunately, though the secrets remained unspoken, they continued to affect relationships and left deep emotional and spiritual wounds. The family secret was subtly influencing family communication and relational dynamics and was the underlying reason for his mother's depression. "My mom learned at a very young age to stuff her emotions and not to deal with pain," Piet said. His mother was in and out of medical facilities throughout his high school and college years, eventually finding some measure of healing.

In college, Piet finally yielded his life to Christ and began growing in his faith. Knowledge of his family's secret and experience working with his mother's depression had helped Piet to understand that even "good people" can find themselves in a bad place, a place they never intended to go. Piet knew firsthand that the pain of the past could continue to affect and shape a person's emotional health, even when the events were intentionally forgotten and the pain buried deep, hidden away. "I firmly believe that an essential part of the discipleship process is the need to talk about emotions," Piet said. "I have always made that a part of my discipleship. It never occurred to me that this was somewhat unusual."

As Piet first entered ministry in the church, it became normal for him to talk openly about emotional health. "The background of my mom's experience gave me permission to speak into the reality of people's lives, their emotions, and how they can be profoundly affected — even today — by the wounds and pain of their past."

After sharing the story of his family and his background in dealing with the hidden wounds of the past, Piet described to the congregation some of the continued impact of the past on his own life. Although many people in the congregation experienced great freedom in their lives after hearing Piet's honest confession, the positive response was by no means universal. Several members were offended by his honesty and felt that it was wrong to air dirty laundry in public. Others rejected the idea that it was necessary to talk about the past before healing could occur. These people believed that it was best to let the past be the past and to simply forget the pain and the mistakes and move on with life. In their minds, talking about these things would never be productive. Several of those who opposed what he was doing were vague about their uneasiness and couldn't quite articulate why they didn't like it. Others lamented, "Our last pastor tanked because of his emotional stuff, and now you are talking about emotions. Shouldn't we just stick to Scripture?"

Despite the criticism, Piet stood by his decision. "Pretending something is not true does not help a person grow. Real change and growth can happen only when the *real* you meets the *real* God." After the sermon series was over, some members left the church. But others, who had heard about his unique message, began coming for the first time. And once again the church grew. Eventually, because of its culture and its community, Woodcrest Chapel became known as a place "for real people and real life."

It Begins with Leadership

So how did the church make this transition? How did the culture change from one of dysfunction and emotional woundedness to one of health and authentic, honest relationships? Piet, as he preached and led, became convinced that the staff and leadership of the church could not lead the way forward in healing and health if they themselves did not make certain core commitments to authenticity and openness in their team relationships.

So Piet and his associate pastor, Rod Casey, set out to cultivate the kind of environment that encouraged openness and honesty during leadership meetings and in daily interactions among the leaders and the staff. They knew they needed to model what it means to be real if they expected others to be real. They needed to be honest about their struggles and their daily journeys of faith if they expected others to do the same. Piet was convinced that dealing openly with one's emotions is simply part of a healthy discipleship process. He also believed that refusing to share what is really happening leads to emotional barriers that keep people from growing in their relationship with God. So he encouraged the leaders and the staff to bring what was happening in their lives into their team relationships.

Piet wanted to create the kind of environment where people would thrive, a place where they would want to stick around for the long haul. But Piet also realized that not everyone would agree with his new approach. And he was right. Some people readily embraced what he was saying, while others checked out. The latter were uncomfortable with the touchy-feely aspects of relational openness and were more comfortable working in a business environment than in a healthy family environment. So as the leadership culture continued to shift and grow at Woodcrest, several leaders self-selected out of the church, recognizing that they were no longer a good fit. "If they don't want to deal with their stuff, they won't stay long on the staff team," Piet said, "but if they are looking to grow, there is no better place to do so than a healthy church family."

Piet soon realized that the people who had chosen to remain on the team and were doing effective ministry were those who had bought into his open style of leadership. As time passed, the new practices of honesty and transparency on his leadership team developed into habits and became the "new normal" for team dynamics at the church. Now, after a decision is made or a course of action is chosen, the team — without prompting — stops, reflects, and asks honestly, "Why did that work or not work?" Eventually the leadership team pulled together many of the principles they were operating under and developed a document titled "Twenty-Five Highly Disputable Principles for Creating a Healthy Corporate Culture." This document was the catalyst for a book titled *Building Ministry Teams That L.A.S.T.*, which focuses on four key principles of team dynamics:

1. *Losing regularly.* This first key principle recognizes that building teams requires leaders to discern and live out their calling within the context of community with other passionate leaders, not in a vacuum. This means relinquishing control and influence to other team leaders (who will make decisions that we don't always agree with). At Woodcrest, effective leadership

is not autocratic. John 3:30 illustrates the wisdom of this principle, but that doesn't mean it is an easy one to apply! Conflict will arise as a team works together. The key to "losing regularly" is living with nothing hidden. All members are given a vocabulary for talking openly about their areas of concern (including their nonnegotiables) without sacrificing relationship. This team adheres to the principle that either the group will process emotions and conflict fully or the team dynamics will become destructive. They would rather lose regularly in the area of control and influence than suffer defeat as a result of unresolved conflict.

2. *Acknowledging problems early.* Piet and his team are not naive; they realize that a team approach to ministry is not for everyone. They are comfortable when people self-select themselves off the team. He also acknowledges the tendency to try to retain unhappy team members — sometimes to the detriment of all. Careful attention to clarity of communication, saying *everything* — including the difficult 10 percent of conversation that most people leave unsaid — and finding ways to use qualifiers like "I may not know everything, but it appears to me ..." to communicate trust and appropriate self-awareness all help to address and solve problems. If teams are committed to addressing problems early, it is helpful to develop a process for doing so that builds trust and doesn't complicate the resolution with unclear communication.

3. *Sharing feelings appropriately.* The capacity to identify feelings and not ignore, minimize, or spiritualize what is going on with us is important in the life of every maturing leader. Ministry is a unique environment; special vigilance is key as we seek to deal with our emotional issues and attend to ministry matters.

4. *Taking both sides.* In keeping with Woodcrest's principle to live openly and honestly as a community, the

team respects the "two sides" of each individual. The things we most love about each other bring with them a flip side — those parts that irritate us. If we remove the irritants, we may sacrifice the things that we most cherish and that make us most effective in our calling. This principle teaches teams to build with the flip side in mind.

As the staff and leadership began to live these principles, the culture of the church moved from pretense and buried emotion to a place of healing, acceptance, authenticity, grace, and safety. It didn't take long for people who were struggling with issues and losses, who weren't feeling comfortable at other churches, to discover Woodcrest and find hope there.

As I (Liz) have worked with the staff of Woodcrest Chapel, I've been impressed with the fact that they practice what they preach. Their commitment to the principles they verbalize is lived out in their leadership community, their programming, and their relationships with others. The team approach and management style of Woodcrest Chapel leadership have created a culture that is conducive to recovery. Their philosophy of ministry lends itself to attracting members who want to address their problems; practicing the principles that Woodcrest espouses equips church leadership to effectively minister to and provide support for members who ask for help.

It's Not about *Those* People

Woodcrest Chapel is somewhat unique among the churches we are highlighting, in that recovery is front and center in the church culture; it's part of the mainstream. It is not relegated to the periphery of ministry, something only for certain people, the few who struggle. Woodcrest Chapel has managed to become a church that values the recovery process without limiting itself to recovery lingo or unwittingly limiting access to the recovery process to "those people" (the ones with those really *big* problems). They firmly believe that the church is a place for people in process, so it has become part of the new normal to talk about the reality of struggles and broken dreams.

I (Teresa) recognize from my own experience how important it is to make recovery part of the normal life of the church. I was a few months into our recovery ministry start-up at NorthStar Community Church in Richmond, Virginia, when I learned that our fledgling recovery ministry was at risk of becoming marginalized, relegated to a dark corner of the church where only the really bad people would dare go. There are plenty of people out in the community who are desperate enough to travel down the dark steps to a dank room in the basement, so finding people in need of recovery is never a problem. But, I reasoned, if recovery gets stuck on the fringe of church life, if we unwittingly communicate that recovery is for "those people," how will members access the help they need? Church members are the ones who lose out when recovery is sent to the fringe of church life.

One night, after a group meeting, a big burly man with a firm handshake and a sunny smile approached me. "Ma'am, I'd like to give you some feedback, if I may." His southern drawl pulled me in even as his request triggered my anxiety.

"Sure. Tell me more." I mostly meant it.

"We're new to these parts, and I talked to a sweet little woman that works in your church office. Nice as could be, offered me lots of options when I told her I was new in town. Thought you might want to know about it." He paused.

I nodded encouragingly.

"Well, I had heard a rumor at my last AA meeting that y'all might have a recovery meeting at the church. So I just rung your church up and asked. After a few minutes of chitchat, that sweet lady said, 'Sir, we do have one of those meetings. But listening to you, I can just tell that's really not what you need. I think you'd love our contemporary worship service instead. You know that recovery meeting has a lot of *characters* in attendance.'"

He had a laugh that matched his handshake, and he used it to fill the awkward silence. Sober for decades, this kindhearted visitor clearly didn't mind hanging out with "characters." I was grateful that he had the integrity and generosity of spirit to share with me his experience of accessing recovery at our church. I thanked him for his honest feedback and made a mental note to myself: we still had a lot of work to do to change the understanding of recovery in our church!

I took this feedback back to our church staff, and we engaged in dialogue about the unintentional consequences of failing to cast a vision for our staff and congregation about the need for recovery. We coached our volunteers at the welcoming center, educated our entire staff about the need for creating an environment that encourages our members and communities to seek help, used illustrations in sermons that valued the recovery process, and along the way found opportunities to practice what we were preaching when our own families found themselves in need of recovery. We continually discover our need to remind ourselves and others that there is no shame in admitting we have a problem, and that the church is here to help, not judge. Recovery has entered the mainstream culture of the church, and we have become aware that we are *all* characters.

Multiple Avenues of Healing

Recovery ministry at Woodcrest Chapel looks much like most faith-based recovery programs. One night a week, people interested in working on their "issues" head to church, meet in a large group, then break out into small groups. Options include:

- Twelve Step Substance Abuse
- Making Peace with Your Past (helps identify ways the past can affect the present and provides access to hope and healing)
- Moving beyond Your Past (encourages taking personal responsibility for one's "wholeness")
- Conquering Codependency (a twelve-step approach to help identify codependency and move away from the compulsion to fix others)
- Divorce Care
- Shelter from the Storm (help for women recovering from childhood sexual abuse)
- Wounded Heart (help for men recovering from childhood sexual abuse)

The specific types of groups the church offers depends on the availability of leadership and the particular needs of the church and the community at that time. Each group focuses on a single problem, such as divorce, substance abuse, or sexual abuse. A shared experience of suffering is what draws participants into the meeting, but it is shared commitment to healing and finding solutions that keeps them coming back.

Beliefs Are Basic to Life Change

Woodcrest Chapel has taken the time to articulate what they believe and what they are trying to accomplish in their community. They weigh budgeting and staffing changes against their mission, with the conviction that any use of resources that does not go toward the mission is, by definition, a waste of resources. This seems like an obvious step, but it's one that many churches neglect.

The leadership at Woodcrest Chapel has a vision born of a deep conviction that God wants his people to be free, able to talk about their pain and verbally express their emotions. They believe that God intends for every person to have a full, abundant, and joyful life. But they recognize that unresolved issues from the past and compulsions in the present impede the discipleship process, making it impossible to experience the life God intends for us. They also know that God has entrusted his church with the mission of getting out the message of hope that restoration is possible. It is their mission to equip the church with the theological, psychological, and practical resources that create and maintain this Christian approach. It is this intersection of belief and strategic thinking that makes their approach to recovery so effective.

Healthy Leaders = Healthy Church

"Time out. What just happened here?"

"I don't want to talk about it."

"That is not a good-enough answer. It's pretty obvious that something's bothering you. *What do you think that was all about?*"

Embracing brokenness has to be practical. It is common to hear some variation of this conversation during the staff meetings at Woodcrest Chapel as people challenge one another to be honest about how they are feeling and what is wrong.

At Woodcrest Chapel, embracing brokenness is part of every staff member's job description. All staff members are required to take the recovery class Making Peace with Your Past within the first two years of employment. And many staff work through other courses as well. When someone detects that there are issues blocking forward movement in ministry or in a relationship, they don't just move on and get back to the business at hand. They ask questions. These are not meant to be accusations but are intended to serve as opportunities to keep things honest and real and invite growth, even though everyone acknowledges that the process is sometimes painful.

Piet shared that "sometimes people are unaware of their feelings and emotions, so other people on the team will attempt to help them sort things out." Piet's commitment to developing a team of staff members who are willing (and able) to resolve their issues provides a training ground that prepares staff for helping the whole congregation resolve their personal roadblocks to intimacy with God. Wrestling with their own emotional booby traps enables staff members to speak authentically of growing in faith, not just preach and teach on what the Scriptures say disciples should or should not do.

Staff meetings at this church are all about practicing what is preached — sometimes to the point of annoyance. It's not unusual to hear a staff member at Woodcrest express with equal parts lament and laughter, "Can't we have just one meeting where we don't have to talk about our feelings?"

Ministers are busy people. The tyranny of the urgent encourages ministry teams to stick to the surface — tasks and "to do's," coordinating use of rooms, keeping the calendar updated, and organizing staff vacations so that staffing needs are covered for the Christmas Eve service, the Easter Sunday service. But it is this willingness to "go there" that creates such an authentic recovery-rich environment. In his book *Building Ministry Teams That L.A.S.T,* Piet writes, "Ministry is different.... Ministry first and foremost is soul work — not just as it relates to other people's souls, but primarily as it relates to our own souls. A minister with an empty and depleted soul is in reality not a minister at all. It may appear odd to see it put this way, but the chief objective in Christian service is to be a genuine Christian yourself first and always. Therefore, it is the primary responsibility of every minister to attend to his or her own soul first. When doing ministry as a team, we also have a responsibility to serve one another by attending to each other's soul development."[11]

Piet writes that a healthy team must have healthy players — members who can resolve their issues, whether those are internal or interpersonal. What Piet discovered in his quest for a highly functioning team was that it wasn't enough for the team to just want it. They needed decent team-building practices.

According to Rod Casey, the associate pastor who advised Piet against sharing his story that first Sunday, another way in which healthy teams know and embrace each other's brokenness is through a shared vocabulary. After years of trial and error, Piet and Rod have developed a vocabulary that works for them. For example, they refer to brokenness as the "dark side." Piet said, "If we as leaders are going to influence the culture of the church, we need to start with ourselves, as leaders. We can't expect our people to be something we refuse to be. Recovery is born of the life you are doing together with your leadership team. It's about how you are able to help each other navigate their stuff so that it becomes a core value in the church. Unless you are willing to have those kinds of conversations with your team, your preaching or teaching won't have much influence on the church."

In recovery, leaders lead the way, both in what they do and in what they say.

An Integrated Ministry

"Everybody needs recovery," according to Rod Casey. "Mild dysfunction (family-of-origin stress) is harder to spot than acute dysfunction but equally as destructive. Eighty-five percent of children of alcoholics feel abandoned, which we understand, but 35 percent of children of busy pastors also feel abandoned. We need ministries that help the whole spectrum of people."

Abandonment and other unresolved issues in the past hinder people's ability to experience the life God intended. These issues do not need to be judged by degree of difficulty; they simply require resolution. Rod clarifies his perspective on recovery at Woodcrest when he says, "Our default definition of recovery is not about managing our addictions; it's about embracing our brokenness." Instead of limiting recovery ministry to particular issues like drug addiction or alcoholism, they keep the broad definition in mind — embracing brokenness. This opens up the conversation so that every church member can talk about it.

Because the assumption at the church is that *everyone* has issues and that unresolved issues hinder the discipleship process, the staff at Woodcrest consider it "mission critical" that these assumptions are taken into account as they strategize how to best serve their congregation. Rod's wife, Julie, is part of the team that oversees and develops the recovery ministry at the church. As a result of Piet's first message series and her own ongoing anxiety attacks, Julie is now experiencing the grace and healing she desperately wants for others. "We desire for people to remove the emotional barriers that hinder their relationships with God and others," she said. "Woodcrest Chapel exists to help connect people to God." She is passionate about her part in the bigger picture. If emotional barriers are a problem, she and her team want to provide a safe place to grow.

Julie is encouraged and enabled by her church's integrated approach to recovery. "I know that most people in our church embrace the process of restoration and want to know how they can help." Julie can say with confidence to a first-time visitor in the Thursday night recovery program, "You need to be at church in a weekend service and you need to be in a recovery group and midweek ministry, since those messages and experiences are going to help you in your recovery and in the process of getting better. These are equally safe places to be who you are and where you are on your recovery journey."

Slower Is Faster

A need alone does not elicit an emergency response to launch a recovery or support group. Piet's commitment to "taking the slow road"[12] and wisely testing the organizational fit before adding team members has encouraged Julie to take the same approach in her own ministry. "For three years I knew we needed to start a grief recovery group, but we didn't have the leadership to do so. It was hard, but I didn't force the issue. I prayed and waited," she admits. Recently a qualified, able leader has expressed an interest in starting this group. "Although the waiting is hard," she says, "I know our priority is people, not programs. It is hard when the need seems so urgent, but I've learned the value of living by our principles."

Julie and her team are energized as they continue to serve in the area of recovery. They are bolstered by sermons, a shared staff vision, core principles, and organizational decisions that work collaboratively with what they are doing on the recovery ministry team. Does it work perfectly? Of course not. Recently the leaders at Woodcrest were dismayed by the discovery that one of their key volunteers was secretly engaged in immoral behavior. Pastors dread hearing that they have a leader who has a hidden, unresolved sin issue. It can be a disheartening and stressful revelation, one that requires tough leadership decisions and wisdom in communicating with the affected teams and families involved in the crisis. But at Woodcrest Chapel, a restoration process is already in place.

In keeping with their belief that all people have issues that need resolution, a restoration team has been formed to tackle the inevitable stumbling that is part of the human condition and to mediate its potential harming effects on the church community. The team is not composed of a group of specialists. Instead, anyone on staff may be qualified to participate on the restoration team. Selecting the particular team members for a given individual is based on the situation and that individual, considering the question, What is best for the one needing restoration? This approach spreads out the intensity of the work among the entire staff, rather than relying on just a few with specialized degrees. It avoids compartmentalizing the process and creates a spirit of oneness, not only with the staff but with the church members as well. "The process is always driven by the principles we live by," Julie said.

One thing is clear, though: restoration is not punishment. "Our goal is to reconcile the person to the community and, ideally, restore them to serve as they had before," Julie says. This kind of education, intervention, and accountability provides a safe environment that makes having and resolving issues a church problem, not just a reason to shuttle someone off to the sidelines, leading to further isolation and reducing the chance that the offending and the broken will get the support and help they so clearly need.

Summing up his perspective on recovery ministry, Rod shared candidly with us, "What I love about our ministry is our willingness to embrace the realities of the fall, not just the benefits of the cross. A holistic Christian worldview leans into our 'flesh patterns' to maximize our growth in Christlikeness and to avoid the Enemy's schemes. Some things only heaven will fix. Until then we are wise to continually stay in touch with our recovery need while living in light of our identity in Christ."

Questions for Reflection and Discussion

1. Piet noticed certain unhealthy communication patterns and high emotion from leaders and staff at Woodcrest. What are some of the communication patterns — positive and negative — in your leadership?

2. What do those patterns reveal to you?

3. How do your leaders or staff resolve conflict or sort things out?

4. Describe the types of dysfunction, both mild and severe, that you have seen or experienced.

5. What terms are used in your church when it comes to areas of recovery, brokenness, healing, sin, or confession?

chapter three

CANCER, ADDICTION, AND A MEXICAN DUMP
Henderson Hills Baptist Church

> On occasion you experience that indescribable moment
> when you know the Lord has spoken. I'm not trying to
> sound too mystical, but that is exactly what happened to me.
> — *Pastor Dennis Newkirk*

DENNIS NEWKIRK IS SENIOR PASTOR of Henderson Hills
Baptist Church, a church with a weekend attendance of 7,400 in
Edmond, Oklahoma. Edmond is a city known for its friendly down-
home atmosphere and was beginning a growth spurt as an upper
middle-class bedroom community when Dennis began as senior
pastor in 1992. Over the fifteen years that he has been at Henderson Hills, the church has more than tripled in size. Not only has
his teaching helped the church's growth, but so has his transparency, an important quality in leaders who have recovery ministries.
These days, Dennis teaches with great humility and inclusivity as
a fellow traveler who is also learning along with the congregation,
but it wasn't always that way. In fact, it took many years as a pastor
before Dennis paid close attention to the reality of brokenness in his
congregation, in his own life, and in the world and began to develop
a recovery ministry at Henderson Hills.

In 1999, three things occurred that led Dennis to become more transparent and open to the new thing that God wanted to do through Henderson Hills. First, Dennis was diagnosed with cancer. Doctors caught it early and the cancer was successfully removed with no complications. The prognosis was excellent! But the future was still not bright for Dennis. He was anything but optimistic, and as time went on, he became more depressed, more fearful, and more anxious. He was fearful of a recurrence of the cancer even though he had been declared cancer free. He became preoccupied with and controlled by his fears.

While outwardly he kept up appearances, emotionally and spiritually he was a train wreck. "I was sidelined by a totally unrealistic fear and anxiety. How could such incredibly good news about my future lead to this disabling anxiety?" Dennis went to his doctor and was repeatedly reassured, "Listen, Dennis, there is nothing to worry about. Your cancer is not going to come back." But the confident words of his doctor did nothing to alleviate his anxiety. He went to the elders, and they told him to just trust Jesus. While Dennis wanted to trust Jesus and be free from his fear, the darkness remained. He met with a psychologist. The psychologist was somewhat helpful, but still Dennis was not getting better. He'd read the Bible and think, "It's not working for me anymore." As a pastor, a spiritual leader of others, he could no longer figure out for himself how to apply the things he was reading in the Bible. "My inability to get better and overcome my fears began to shake my faith," Dennis says.

During this time of personal struggle, Dennis reflected on a recent mission trip to Matamoras, Mexico. On his visit to Mexico, he had met Rita Hernandez, a sixteen-year-old girl who lived in an old shack at the rat-infested city dump. Rita spent her days sifting through the trash and debris, looking for pieces of scrap metal. After she had collected enough scrap, she sold the metal to buy food. In addition to her poor living conditions, Rita had also sustained a life-altering injury in her early childhood. She had experienced such a severe break to her leg that it caused one foot to be permanently rotated 180 degrees in the opposite direction of her other foot. Not only was this an unsightly malady; it made her attempts to navigate through the dump a constant struggle. As Dennis spent time talking with

Rita, he found himself deeply moved by her situation. He found that he could no longer simply preach the good news and then just walk away. Even after returning home, he continued to think about her and wondered whether there was something more he and the church could be doing to help.

A third situation rocked Dennis's world that year. A family member approached him to share a struggle with alcohol. The ensuing discussion revealed that some deep wounds from childhood had manifested into an addiction. Dennis was shocked at the devastating effect that an addiction was having on someone from his own family, and it forced him to pause and wonder, "What did I miss? What caused this person, who is so involved in the church, to enter into a secret life of addiction? How many others in our church are in the same situation? Where are the resources available to help these hurting people — to help people like me?"

Dennis knew that something was missing from the ministry of Henderson Hills Baptist Church.

Finding Guidance

As Dennis pondered his baseless fears, the overwhelming needs of Rita in Mexico, and the shock of an addiction in his family, he began seeking God for the answers that had eluded him. For many years he had been finding God's direction through the alignment of three things: practicing spiritual disciplines, his personal experience, and times of personal encounter with God.

All three of these converged one morning as he was driving to the church. He was listening to the book of Luke on CD in his car. Two verses stood out to him with unusual clarity that morning. It was as if he had never really understood them before. As the narrator spoke these words from Luke 4:18 – 19, something subtly shifted in Dennis's heart, and immediately it became clear to him what he needed to do. The narrator read, "The Spirit of the Lord is on me, because he has anointed me to preach good news to the poor. He has sent me to proclaim freedom for the prisoners and recovery of sight for the blind, to release the oppressed, to proclaim the year of the Lord's favor."

Dennis was about two blocks from church when he sensed that

God was speaking to him directly from these verses. And by the time he arrived at church, he knew exactly what God was calling Henderson Hills to become. "God created a vision in my mind for the future of Henderson Hills," he said. He walked into the worship center and began work on what God had revealed to him. The Ministries of Jesus Clinic was birthed that day, and Henderson Hills Baptist Church has never been the same.

"I realized," Dennis said, "that when Jesus read these verses from Isaiah 61, he was talking about *his* ministry. He was talking about preaching the gospel. He was anointed to bring the good news — the gospel — to the poor. He talked about giving release to the captives and giving sight to the blind and setting free those who were held captive, oppressed, or downtrodden. Luke 4 describes the kind of ministry that Jesus did and the kind of ministry he wants us to have today, a ministry like the one Jesus himself practiced. If Jesus has truly left his Spirit to live in us, then he has also left us here to do his work.

"Jesus ministered to the whole person — spiritually, physically, and emotionally. The Lord wants to bring healing to the whole person, and I realized that was exactly the kind of church we needed to become. If we were really his body, why should we settle for anything less? Whether a person is ill or is dealing with an addiction, such things affect the whole person, and we needed to minister to the whole person — body, mind, and spirit."

A picture formed in his mind, a vision of how to truly minister to the whole person, not in a segmented fashion but in a holistic way. Henderson Hills would no longer be just a place that talked about the ministry of Jesus. It would be a place that did the ministry of Jesus. Henderson Hills would not just tell others what Jesus had done; it would also be a place where people could experience what Jesus is still doing today — healing lives and setting people free from the power of sin.

Those who are called to lead God's people should also note that Dennis made many of these tough decisions in the midst of his struggle with depression and anxiety. Ultimately, it was his own suffering that served as a catalyst for the changes in ministry at the church. God's revelation to Dennis did not come *after* he had gotten his act together; instead, it arose from the rubble of his internal confusion. In the midst of his fear of dying, his doubts about helping others find their freedom, and the despair he felt while preaching the gospel to a teenage girl with a badly deformed leg, a new vision for ministry was born in his heart and in the life of the church.

Ministries of Jesus Clinic Unfolds

Dennis had been given a vision. He knew that Henderson Hills would be a place of healing. But what form would it take? Dennis began by gathering a group of people not because of their positions in the church but simply to create a mix of mature and older Christians along with a few younger believers who were growing in their faith. He invited a couple of physicians, several businesspeople, and others with various vocations. His goal was to bring people from several different backgrounds, with different skills and gifts, together in a ministry of collaboration. This spirit of collaboration continues to be reflected through an attitude of humility and a willingness to learn from others, an attitude that characterizes the staff at Henderson Hills. He told the group his story, sharing what God had placed on his heart, and then asked them, "Do you know of a place where a person can come for the healing of the body, soul, and spirit?" No one there could think of such a place. Physicians know how to treat people with physical needs, psychologists focus on the emotional and mental needs, and pastors most often address spiritual issues. Dennis pointed out to the group that all these people do their work independently of one another. But is it really possible to separate these three areas of our lives? If a person suffers physically, they also suffer emotionally and spiritually. Emotional suffering manifests itself physically and spiritually. Regardless of the issue, the problem will impact every aspect of life in some manner.

Dennis and his newly formed group devised a plan. They birthed a vision for a clinic that would address an individual's threefold needs. When a person entered their facility, they would be evaluated in all three areas: physical health, mental and emotional health, and spiritual health. Working together, a team of experts would then put together a plan. Not only that, but they would offer their services at no charge so that patients would need no insurance. They wanted anyone — regardless of their financial situation — to be free to get the help they needed. As clients would arrive, each one would go through an evaluation process, always with the understanding that the focal point of the healing experience would be spiritual healing of the individual. The group was energized by the vision, and several physicians and other medical personnel volunteered their time. Others invested time to help run the office and assist in administrative duties. Pharmacy salespeople donated medications.

Within three months of articulating their dream, the Ministries of Jesus Clinic opened in a strip mall near the church. One of their first transformational endeavors was visiting the garbage dump in Matamoras and bringing Rita to the States for a leg operation to reset her broken and deformed foot. Since the operation, Rita has been able to graduate from high school and has now started college. She has also become an avid follower of Jesus.

Adding Recovery Ministry

As the clinic evolved, the church leaders sensed the need for a specific type of ministry. It made sense to them that if they were going to focus on the whole person, part of that ministry would include a way to help "set the captives free" from the addictions that were devastating their lives. They decided to start a ministry for recovery and made it an integral part of the Ministries of Jesus vision. "The concept that addictions contain not only a disease element that needs to be addressed but also a spiritual element that relates to obedience to Christ is a vital part of the ministry that needs to be understood," Dennis explained. To begin the ministry, they began to study the Scriptures and out of their study developed a theology of recovery that guides their practice (see appendix D).

For six years, Henderson Hills led their recovery ministry through the efforts of several talented volunteer and part-time leaders, but eventually Dennis sensed that the church was ready to take the next step and hire a full-time director of recovery. Today Chuck Robinson serves in that role and oversees the step studies[13] three to four nights a week as well as a weekly large group gathering called Recovery

Flock, which focuses on either a Bible study topic or a book study on a recovery issue. On Wednesday evenings, the ministry offers two additional groups: one for spouses of those dealing with sexual addiction and another for men addressing their sexual addiction issues.

Chuck's own journey of recovery gives him a unique passion for and insight into the work he oversees, but it took many years for him to reach that point. In 1982, Chuck began his own recovery process from addiction, and in 1988 he felt God's call to minister to others in recovery. During a sermon one morning at Henderson Hills, Pastor Dennis shared with the congregation his hope for a full-time leader: "Wouldn't it be neat if someone stepped forward to become a recovery minister in our church?" At that moment, Chuck thought, "Maybe that's me!" It was another twenty years before Chuck was ready to take on the important role of leading the recovery ministries at the church, but his experience and passion are evident to all who are served by the clinic. It was certainly worth the wait!

As we've talked with churches around the country, we've noticed that Chuck's story is not unique. It's a recurring theme in many recovery ministries. Repeatedly, recovery leaders articulate to us how their spiritual journeys, their struggles and sufferings, have been used by God as an impetus for acquiring the experience, strength, and hope to help others.

Be Real about Your Doubts and Failures

Everyone goes through difficult times. Everyone experiences broken relationships, setbacks, failures, and disappointments. But these heartbreaks can serve as the foundation for ministering to others. Leaders who are willing to enter into the pain of darkness and loss and resolve their emotional wounds are able to help others walk into light. By allowing God to meet us where we are and to walk with us, we can develop sensitive hearts toward others who are in need of God's presence as much as they need God's answers. Second Corinthians 1:3 – 4 is a helpful reminder of this truth: "All praise to the God ... of all healing counsel! He comes alongside us when we go through hard times, and before you know it, he brings us alongside someone else who is going through hard times so that we can be there for that person just as God was there for us" (MSG).

What organizations such as Alcoholics Anonymous and those who serve in recovery ministry learn is that it is frequently through failures, setbacks, and pain that we gain the experience we need to truly be helpful to others. The doubts that we struggle through today may become the tools we need to minister to someone's need tomorrow. "Trouble" is the experience needed to minister to the troubled and broken of the church and the community. Leaders can be restorers only as they acknowledge their own brokenness and allow God to restore them. There can be no environment of healing grace if there isn't also an environment of brokenness and a willingness to deal with sin.

People learn to trust God in difficult circumstances because they have seen others trust God in difficult circumstances. Transparency about our own struggles creates an environment where people are no longer afraid to share the truth about their unresolved issues. In this sense, suffering becomes a blessing, a training ground for authentic ministry to others.

As the leader of recovery ministries, Chuck is quick to praise the leadership of the church for creating an environment that accepts the reality that people who walk with God are still broken and sinful people in need of God's daily grace and healing. "From the top leadership to all those in the church, this awareness frees us to accept those who are broken and seeking God. At Henderson Hills Baptist Church, we don't shoot our wounded, especially if they happen to be our ministers. We are 110 percent committed to not marginalizing those in need of transformation," Chuck said.

He contrasts this attitude with his early experiences in recovery, when people with substance abuse issues (like him) were asked by their churches to go out and "find a place, like Alcoholics Anonymous, to help them." The thinking at that time was clear: after you're better, you can come back to church and serve.

Everyone at Henderson Hills recognizes that they are still in process and that perfection is reserved for Jesus alone. Chuck shares why they not only tolerate brokenness but also welcome it: "We tend to despise our spiritual brokenness. We hate it. But God sees it differently. Not only does God *not* despise our spiritual brokenness; God sees it as a kind of worship, as a kind of sacrifice. God understands how painful it is to say no to our idolatrous attachments, and God understands how difficult it is for us to let them go. God also recognizes the spiritual maturity that is being shaped within us during this difficult process."[14]

[margin note: Not so sure about the wording of this...]

He acknowledges that Henderson Hills' recovery ministry is not just for "those people." "People in churches seem to get the idea that 'they' out there are sick, and 'we' in here have it all together. I was very emphatic with our people that this is why Jesus complained about the Pharisees — seeing themselves without sin and looking upon everyone else with judgment. That was, and still is, immoral, unethical, unbiblical, and extremely unchristian."[15]

Church members are availing themselves of the resources of the recovery programs. They have discovered that although loving God is not an antidote for difficult family issues (it's good to remember that most suffering is relational), Henderson Hills is a place where it is safe to love God and get honest about their problems. Suffering is viewed not through the lens of judgment or shame but through the lens of grace and growth. Asking for help is seen not as a sign of weakness but as a sign of hope and strength. People have an eager expectancy that change can happen, especially at church, *because* of the church. They have found a bridge to God's grace through a community of love and acceptance.

Grace Is a Place

"Many of us understand grace as a theological position. And it is!" writes Dr. Bill Thrall. "Undeserved, unending, unearned, unwavering, grace is God's inexhaustible love and absolute acceptance of us, coupled with his unabashed delight in us. Grace brings us adoption into God's family, a new identity, a new life, new power, new capacity, and God's full protection — with absolutely no strings attached! But grace is much more than a theological position. Equally and simultaneously, grace is an actual environment, a realm, a present-tense reality that weaves around and through every moment of even our worst day. God's gift of grace continuously and always surrounds us."[16]

God's grace is needed for more than just the forgiveness of sin. Dallas Willard cautions us against a narrow understanding of grace: "The interpretation of grace as having only to do with guilt is utterly false to biblical teaching and renders spiritual life in Christ unintelligible."[17] Those who serve in the recovery ministry at Henderson Hills believe that God's grace is meant to provide more in the life of believers than just the removal of a particular affliction or sin, No longer defined by their dysfunction, those who follow through with the recovery process also come to embrace the gospel and discover who they are in Christ. They accept the righteousness of Christ and are freed from the burden of creating their own identity. Instead, they are free to serve others as they claim their true, God-created identity in Christ.

Kim Swyden, executive pastor at Henderson Hills, is eager to point out, "This does not mean we are light on sin." He believes that it's easy to assume or take for granted the "power of the gospel" and then fail to grapple with the ongoing daily struggles. Salvation is more than just a provision for eternity. "We are provoked to take God's saving grace seriously," he said. "We believe that salvation is for eternity *and* for our lives now! We are convinced that it was never God's intent for churches to wait for people to get cleaned up before they would be accepted. This conviction has changed the way we do church. This has changed the way we evaluate 'successful ministry' and helped us actually feel good about what we're doing."

Henderson Hills has created an environment of grace, a place Kim compares to "cool water gushing from an oversized garden hose on a hot summer day. It just keeps making us laugh with delight as it knocks us over, again and again. We swim in it ... we dance in it ... we rejoice in it and are healed by it."

How does this work itself out practically for the staff at the church? Every day, they are reminded to keep what they do personal. Ministry at Henderson Hills is not about launching programs or being "successful." It requires redefining success to acknowledge that moral perfection is not the goal; it's grace-empowered growth into the likeness of Christ. Kim said, "We've discovered that effectiveness is the product of many seemingly inefficient hours with people — talking, listening, drinking coffee, and hanging out. People want to be known, and we must know them if we are to serve each other and minister to each other. The Holy Spirit continues to provoke us to spend time with people, speak into their lives, do the time-intensive work of discipleship, and have the discernment to know when to say to them, 'You're ready; now it's your turn. Serve others!'"

Get Your Hands Dirty

> We have this treasure in jars of clay to show that this all-surpassing power is from God and not from us.
>
> — 2 Corinthians 4:7

Being a recovery minister is something like being a doctor in an emergency room. You never know when the next emergency will come, and sometimes things can get rather unpleasant. When a family discovers that one of their loved ones has an addiction issue, Chuck knows that he may be called into the home in the midst of the crisis. Topics are aired in these stress-filled environments that are often uncomfortable and sometimes dark. Secrets are exposed as a family considers whether they are going to face their issues or wait for the situation to get worse. The elephant in the room — whether it is codependency, workaholism, substance abuse, sexual addiction, gambling, promiscuity, or just about anything — is often acknowledged. An environment like this calls for triage, not a lengthy sermon.

"Families in crisis don't care whether it is your day off. It's like when your house catches fire. The fireman comes no matter the day or time. That's how it is in recovery too," Chuck said. He reluctantly admits that often the role of a first responder to the types of crises that addiction creates isn't well received by those in crisis. But Chuck knows that this too is part of the process, and so he has learned not to take it personally.

Recovery takes time: teaching, mentoring, and counseling. Each of these actions has its place in the recovery process. If a family is to heal from the devastating effects of addiction, more is at stake than sobriety. Recovery involves restoring broken trust, healing marital discord, assisting in financial planning, working out parenting issues, addressing work-related complications, treating depression and anxiety, and much more. Each of these problems can arise at any moment and needs to be addressed at the appropriate time. And to successfully lead to restoration and healing, the process requires a spirit of collaboration and servanthood.

Serving others is at the heart of recovery ministry. Those who serve must guard against serving to reduce their guilt or even in the hope that somehow their good deeds will earn them a return on their investment. Serving is not about gaining approval from others, or even a desperate attempt to earn God's love. Instead, it is a by-product of the gospel, a response of gratitude that overflows from a heart that has been blessed with the gracious love and unmerited acceptance of God.

"I love to see broken people come to Christ and acknowledge the fact that Jesus is the solution," Chuck said. "I love it when hurting people move from total dependence and the belief that they *need* recovery to the place where they realize that the point of all that they have gone through is not their sobriety from whatever they struggle with; instead, it has everything to do with Christ." Recovery is the fruit of a life that has encountered the love, grace, and acceptance of God through Jesus.

Questions for Reflection and Discussion

1. What are some of the problems of life that are present in your congregation?

2. In what ways is your congregation ministering to physical needs?

3. In what ways is your congregation ministering to emotional needs?

4. In what ways is your congregation ministering to spiritual needs?

5. What would it look like to combine and address all three?

6. When speaking in public, do you tend to illustrate points by telling stories of your own current struggles, or do your stories focus on past victories?

chapter four

THE CHURCH, A PLACE OF HOPE AND HELP

Salem Alliance Church

> When we stand at the pulpit and look out over a sea of faces, what we see is a community of hurting individuals who keep hearing the message of grace but do not know how to appropriate it.
>
> — *Pastor Morris Dirks*

MORRIS DIRKS KNEW THAT MANY OF THE PEOPLE in his congregation were dealing with the difficulties and hardships of life. He also knew that they were looking to him with the hope that he would provide some answers for them. But Morris Dirks had come to the sobering realization that "one more sermon on my part will not stem the bleeding I see happening all around me."

Morris saw the need — all around him — but he wasn't sure what to do.

The city of Salem, Oregon, is surrounded by green pastures, fields of flowers, orchards, and vineyards. Salem is the capital city of Oregon and is located in the center of the lush Willamette River Valley, one hour from the Cascade Mountains to the east and an hour from the ocean to the west. Salem Alliance Church is located in the heart of this city.

Morris Dirks was called to be the youth pastor at Salem Alliance in 1988. When Morris arrived at the church, it had a weekend worship attendance of four hundred, a number that has since tripled to twelve hundred on any given Sunday. When Morris started his ministry there, he had no idea that within three short years he would be asked to step up and fill the pulpit as senior pastor. Having had years of experience in youth ministry prior to his arrival at Salem Alliance, Morris had developed a keen eye for recognizing patterns of unhealthy family systems, an appreciation for the hurts and struggles people were dealing with, and an awareness that many individuals and families were burdened by hidden hurts and pain. So when Morris took the pulpit in 1991, he entered his new position knowing full well the condition of the church he was being called to serve.

Disconnect between Pulpit and Pew

But even with this understanding, Morris still noticed a disconnect between what he was telling the congregation about God and about God's power to work in people's lives and the reality of what they were experiencing. "We as pastors have an idealism we hold on to that is contradictory to what we see really happening in the lives of people in our churches," Morris said. He watched people come to church, eager to learn, and then disappear, never to return. He observed others who never missed a Sunday worship service and pretended they were doing great, but they never opened up about their struggles, their hurts, and the shortcomings of their lives. Morris wanted things to change. He saw that many people in the church were suffering through broken relationships, divorce, addictions, and abuse. He wanted to loose people from the chains of their past and help them find freedom from their troubles in Christ.

Morris began questioning a long-held practice: the habit that he and many other pastors had developed of sending people from their churches to professional counselors or therapists. He concluded that there were two major reasons why pastors did this: lack of time and lack of experience. "Pastors just don't have time to meet with individuals every week for months on end. Pastors also don't know what to do. Few pastors are prepared to help with issues of abuse, addictions, and numerous other disorders they are faced with."

Morris believes that his experience is not all that unique. Many pastors are facing similar concerns. For instance, a pastor may preach a series on marriage for two or three months, all the while knowing that there are still marriages falling apart around him. What Morris saw happening in church was discouraging — seeing so many people hurting, and knowing all the time that he wasn't helping them. He said, "We don't have the luxury to meet with people and give them all the time they need. We give them a few weeks, and when we run out of things to say, we tell them, 'Why don't we pray and get back together in six months.' Or we just run out of time and input, and so we refer them to therapists, where they pay hundreds of dollars to get help.

"One by one seems to be an odd way for the church to be dealing with the healing in people's lives. It seems irrational to me that the only way we can really help people is to send them away outside our community. Shouldn't the church be a healing and restorative place? Shouldn't the church be the locus of transformation and not just a place of education and inspiration?" Morris concluded that the church, to really be the church, had to offer more than just hope. It needed to give practical help to hurting people.

Morris had been raised in a strong Christian home and took on a God-directed life at an early age. His personal struggles with sin were neither glaring nor prohibitive to his professional ministry pursuits, yet he was acutely aware that like everyone else, he had his own areas of unresolved hurt, woundedness, and brokenness. His insights, his heart for hurting people, and his burning desire to provide an environment of grace and restoration grew out of his years of experience as well as a passionate conviction that the church should be the first place people think of and go to in order to find sanctuary, help, and healing.

Morris knew that there were more needs in the church than any one person could meet. He also recognized that although counselors were necessary and valuable, many people could not afford to pay the bill for counseling. He feared that only those with enough money would get the help they needed. Morris began to brainstorm what the church could offer to help those who were hurting, both those inside the church and those outside the church who had yet to encounter the saving love of Jesus.

No Jane, No Gain

Jane Wolf was one of the members at Salem Alliance. Morris had gotten to know her over the course of his time at the church, from way back when he was a youth pastor, and he respected her on many levels. She was a kind and caring person, something that was evident in the way she interacted with people. She also had a strong biblical background and a good understanding of the Scriptures, as well as years of ministry experience. She was a pacesetter. Years earlier Jane had directed the women's ministry at another church, caring for women and teaching them the Scriptures. But as she became involved in the lives of women in that church, she began noticing a pattern of quiet desperation in many of the women's hearts. Although she was caring for them to the best of her ability, she still felt inadequate to help them at their deepest level of need.

Long before it was acceptable in much of the church world to study psychology, Jane decided to return to graduate school to get a master's degree in psychology, with the hope of learning how to become a better minister to the women she was serving. But that was in 1977, and at the time her church was not ready to accept that the study of secular psychology had anything positive to contribute to the Christian world. So when Jane's pastor heard about her intentions, he called her husband and told him that he believed studying psychology was a harmful choice and that Jane would be "tainted by the world of psychology." The pastor suggested to Jane's husband that he dissuade her from following this course of action. Believing that she was following God's direction, Jane went against the tide of popular Christian opinion and continued her studies, eventually receiving her degree. She went on to start a private counseling practice, yet another unpopular choice at that time. Even though getting an advanced degree in psychology had run contrary to the current of the church, Jane found her educational background offering her fresh insights into the lives of the women she was serving.

Morris, knowing Jane's background and her willingness to venture into uncharted territory, believed Jane was the person God wanted to use to bring about the change he envisioned for the church. He wanted the church community to become a more accessible place for people to find the help they needed, but he wasn't sure what that would look like. Still, he felt sure that Jane was the one who could help launch it.

Morris wanted to design a program that would be of little to no cost to participants and would teach and counsel people how to work through the problems of addiction, pain, and brokenness together as a church community. He knew that the average sermon or Sunday school class was not able to get down to the deeper issues that were keeping people from living as God intended them to live. "Sermons and Sunday school can offer cognitive input, support through prayer, and friendship, but they don't give you a process for how to really change the way you are thinking, acting, and behaving," he says. Morris was convinced that the church itself needed to go through a process of recovery. Recovery ministry would be able to help individuals who had gotten derailed in a sincere attempt to pursue God and his grace. Recovery ministry could provide guidance, understanding, and a place of safety necessary in order for the process of healing to occur. Morris also believed that God had designed the church to be that place. "Recovery is at the heart of the gospel," he says. "Sin has wounded people on the inside and the outside, and unless we understand how to work through the problems of addiction, pain, and brokenness together, we are not really doing church."

Morris shared his vision with Jane and asked her to consider leaving her private practice to join the paid staff of Salem Alliance. While she agreed to consider it, she knew that she was not entirely prepared to give up the private practice she had developed over years of work for an untested and risky ministry vision. So Jane made a counteroffer. She offered to cut her private practice work down and join the staff on a part-time basis until everyone was convinced that this new venture was really going to work.

Despite her cautious offer, Jane was acutely aware of the need for this type of movement in the church and was as eager as Morris to see things change. Jane knew of the need for this not only because of her education and work experience but also because she herself had lived through the pain and reality of recovery in her family. Jane's sixteen-year-old son had struggled with addictive behaviors, and his struggle had been hers as well, as she lived through the heartbreaking fallout that affects those whose loved ones engage in substance abuse. Jane possessed a profound understanding of what it is like to live in a family in which a loved one struggles with addiction. She understood the personal pain, fear, and disappointment a parent feels, the heartbreak of thinking you have somehow failed your child, and the anger that comes when you start to believe that he or she has recovered, only to have your hopes dashed once again. Sadly, she had also felt the humiliation that comes when you realize that there are people in your own church who not only lack compassion for you but are, in contrast, standing in judgment of you and your family.

Getting Some Skin in the Game

Jane was convinced that unless the church staff understood what the process of authentic recovery entails — what it feels like and what it demands of a person — they could not support the ministry in earnest. They might be willing to give lip service to the ministry or parrot a PR line to promote it, but unless the staff of the church had some "skin in the game," the recovery ministry would fail. For Jane to be involved on a full-time basis, there was one condition: all nine members of the church staff, including Morris, had to first work through the Twelve Steps[18] together as a group. After the staff had completed the Twelve Steps, they would do an open and honest evaluation. If the staff experienced changes in their lives and saw some kind of growth as a result of their working together, and if they were willing to wholeheartedly support the ministry, she would be willing to help launch it. If not, Jane would simply continue to minister and change lives through her private counseling practice. Unless each member of the staff was convinced that the ministry of recovery had something to offer them, Jane knew they would not totally support it. At the very least, the recovery ministry would become a marginalized church program and not influence the mainstream culture of the church. Morris and the staff accepted the proposal and began the program.

Every Tuesday morning for six months, Jane facilitated the journey of recovery for the nine staff through a twelve-step small group study. Working through the Twelve Steps as a group requires real work between the meetings, such as taking a personal inventory or asking forgiveness from those one has hurt. Recovery may help the broken heart or the wounded heart, but it is certainly not for the faint of heart! Courage, authenticity, truth telling, and faith are necessary to the process. Morris set the example for the other staff members in the way he came prepared for each meeting, having taken seriously his assignments. He also led the way in his willingness to be vulnerable and honest, asking good questions. At the end of the six-month experience, he conducted an anonymous evaluation by staff participants and found that there was unanimous agreement. The staff at Salem Alliance Church gave their wholehearted endorsement to the launch of a ministry of recovery, and Jane was hired full-time to lead this new endeavor.

New Beginnings

Jane's passion to help people appropriate God's grace and find healing for their wounds burns today with the same bright intensity it did when she began her pioneering work decades ago. Though her small size and cheery smile give her the appearance of a woman ready to share the latest photos of her grandchildren, beware of your first impressions! Underneath her gentle exterior lies the heart of a lioness. In her book *Stepping Out with Hope and Healing for a Hurting World*,[19] Jane shares glimpses of her own frustration as she recounts times when she pounded her desk with her fists in aggravation at the struggle involved in counseling and caring for broken people. Through it all, however, she has remained steadfast.

Jane is desperately devoted to a cause and not a program, and she refuses to allow recovery ministry to be marginalized. She writes, "Grasp the heart and soul of what it takes for broken people to walk into wholeness, because when that heart and soul are in place, hurting people will find lasting healing, as well as the healer."[20] Her unwavering commitment and her church's willingness to follow her lead make her an excellent and realistic guide for churches seeking an innovative approach to recovery ministry today.

Keep It Real

It's not a coincidence that the driving force behind the recovery movement at Salem Alliance Church is a former youth pastor. Hanging out with teenagers means always keeping the message real. Morris Dirks had often found himself stuck in a van with fifteen youths headed on a retreat, listening in as they shared their struggles and gossiped about their parents. So when he transitioned from the youth pastor to the senior pastor, he found that he knew things about the people in his church that he wished he could forget, intimate knowledge about pain, suffering, betrayal, and broken lives, and he had a deep awareness of his inability to effect change through his preaching and the normal church programs.

Morris made a courageous move when he chose to acknowledge the problem and wrestle with the incapacity of the church to help those struggling with broken relationships, bad marriages, poor parenting, addiction issues, and other mental-health conditions. He asked the hard questions: Why aren't we addressing the real problems of our community? Where is evidence of the transformation that is preached and promised from the pulpit on a weekly basis? How can we change?

He also refused to whitewash the truth about the state of his congregation or back down on the nature of their calling and responsibility. Morris believed that the church was supposed to be a place that offered both hope and healing, and he wasn't willing to abdicate his responsibilities as a leader or to make excuses. Instead, he sought to change the church from the inside out. This required being honest about his own (and the church's) limitations. It required a dose of humility as he prepared for the necessary changes.

Start Smart

Starting smart is key not just to launching but also to sustaining an effective recovery ministry. Jane Wolf has developed several "smart start" principles that she believes have enabled Salem to weather the test of time:

- *Start small.* If the staff and key lay volunteers are willing to live in an environment of brutal honesty (something that all participants in a recovery program are taught to value), then it's important to keep in mind that any start-up ministry has lots to learn. Particularly in the field of recovery, where many participants will walk in with stories of abandonment and abuse, there is no need to pile on more heartache by starting something the church cannot support long-term. Make sure that sustainability of a mission is always discussed frankly. New ventures are inherently exciting and create lots of buzz and enthusiasm. But this is a mission that requires the stamina of a marathoner, not a sprinter. Start small, go slow.

- *Acknowledge ignorance when appropriate.* Morris sought out Jane to provide him with the experience and expertise he was willing to admit that he lacked. He had vision, authority, and willingness to advance the cause. He added to that a director he could trust because she had the passion, preparation, expertise, and leadership skills to put feet to his dream.

- *Develop relationships with like-minded people and work collaboratively.* Build a team of people whose hearts beat for the same things. Recovery ministry taxes the resources of churches and their leaders, so collaboration with other churches may make a recovery ministry possible by pooling resources. One church may not have all that it needs to run a well-rounded recovery ministry, but three churches might be able to create a strong presence in their community. It isn't necessary for every church to host its own program, but it is essential that every community have access to this kind of resource. Programs like Alcoholics Anonymous, Narcotics Anonymous, Overeaters Anonymous, and Codependents Anonymous have functioned effectively for many years. Acquainting both the recovery ministry and the church with these local secular recovery programs can boost the "serve potential" of a start-up ministry. They offer specialized skill sets, such as running sustainable, effective small groups or developing strong mentors, that churches can learn from.

- *Value people over programs.* Salem Alliance launched a recovery ministry because they valued their people and believed God when he promised to heal and transform them. This was not a thinly veiled attempt to increase church enrollment or a way for the pastor to manage his workload by passing his most wounded (and time-consuming) congregants off to someone else. This decision was not made in reaction to members searching for answers in the office of a therapist instead of the church. Morris and his staff were convinced that the church was responsible to bring God's message of hope and healing to the community, and they took action to rectify the situation when they saw they were failing in their mission.

- *Believe the good news.* Because Salem Alliance believed that the heart of the gospel is Christ's plan for transformation, they were fully convinced and committed, willing to go to any length to create a culture that facilitated the process. Unwilling to make excuses for the disconnect between what they were teaching and what they were witnessing in the lives of their people, folks like Jane Wolf set out to discover how to minister more effectively. This foray into a world of learning beyond that of her denomination was met with resistance by more traditional thinkers. But Jane believed God and refused to settle for the status quo. This type of gritty determination is required for anyone wanting to serve hurting people. Working in a recovery ministry is dirty work. Some days the only thing that will keep the recovery ministry team going is their belief that God will fulfill his promises to heal and restore the brokenhearted.

People Follow, so Lead Wisely

The lead pastor and the governing body of a church need not only to support the mission; they must also model the change they seek to bring about. If a church wants to solve the problem of pulpit-and-pew disconnect, the staff must go first and lead the way. When Salem Alliance explored the idea of a restoration and recovery ministry, Jane challenged them to carefully count the cost. She asked the staff to sacrifice personally by committing to their own recovery program. This willingness to study, learn, and do all this as a team helped the church make an informed decision when they decided to launch the recovery ministry. When referring someone to the program, the staff can speak from their own experience. They believe there is value in the process, because *they* value the experience.

A wise leader is also an honest leader. The Salem staff elevated the value of honesty by daring to work through the Twelve Steps themselves. Looking back, the leaders at Salem now see that this was the genesis for creating a culture of honesty in the entire church, not just a new ministry program. Although not all of the recovery ministries use a twelve-step model, every recovery ministry is committed to creating an environment of honesty, a place where people can share without shame, pretense, or fear of public exposure. When leaders practice honesty, it is easier for congregants to follow their lead. And while it is possible to offer recovery ministries in a way that keeps them at the margins of the church, this is not something the leaders at Salem would advise. Leaders who practice recovery principles in their own lives validate the journey, bridging the gap between flowery sermons and real-life application.

Students Are Great Teachers

Most recovery ministry leaders agree — they learn more from their students than their students learn from the ministry. Jane and her team are no exception. When she learned that addiction had broken through the doors of her own home, Jane was equipped to practice the very principles she had been teaching others for years. Surveying recovery ministries across the country shows that no family is immune to the addiction experience — even families who work in the field of recovery. Even the best doctors' children get sick sometimes.

The value of running ministries that teach and practice honesty in all areas is that leaders are embraced and not ostracized when problems come knocking on their own doors. This is a great gift that recovery ministry offers to churches and their staff. Many pastors regularly live in a state of unease, fearful that problems in their families will disqualify them from their calling or get them fired from their jobs.

The principles that drive recovery ministry are the foundation of a healthy church community because they provide solid, biblical ways to deal with the inevitable failings of sinful human beings. People mess up. Kids get into trouble. Marriages go through seasons of strain. Some of the best resources available to church staff are accessible through the local recovery ministry.

The nature of the work done in recovery ministries requires that everyone attaches great importance to the learning process. People in need of recovery won't experience much life transformation until they embrace a willingness to change. As healing occurs in families once rocked by the devastation that dysfunction and addiction cause, witnesses to the process are encouraged and inspired in their own lives. Churches like Salem Alliance are inspired by the stories they hear from families who were once lost but now have hope and have experienced God's healing.

That said, we also need to recognize that not all stories will have a happy ending. Desperate people wander in every week through the doors of a recovery ministry. Some show up high; others turn up looking for a handout. Most have tried a lot of ways to get sober and to find help, with little success. Not everyone who comes to visit is willing to stay and do the hard work of asking God to remove the shortcomings and defects of character that have caused such devastation and loss. There are no easy answers or shortcuts to a renewed life, and this can prove quite draining to those leading the ministry. Jane's longevity in the field is attributable in large part to some advice she provides at the conclusion of her book *Stepping Out*: "Remember, this is God's work. Put yourself in a place where you can hear his voice, then follow his leading."[21]

That's a word of wisdom we all need to remember.

Questions for Reflection and Discussion

1. Morris Dirks' experience as a youth minister and Jane Wolf's experience as a counselor provided insight and a good platform on which to build a recovery ministry. What other professions, education, or experiences might also give a foundation to a restorative ministry?

2. Lack of time and lack of experience are two reasons pastors often give for referring people to professional counselors and therapists. When do you most often refer people to professional help and why?

3. What is your level of preparedness in helping people who are dealing with issues of abuse, addictions, disorders, or struggles?

4. Who are some of the pacesetters in your congregation? What is their ministry experience and passion?

5. What other churches in your community offer recovery-type ministries or twelve-step programs?

chapter five

IT'S ALL ABOUT THEM, NOT ABOUT US

Bon Air Baptist Church

> We were called to be pastors, not to be the Human Resource guy, to massage the church budget, or to edit the church newsletter. Most of us began with that prompting from God's Spirit, who said, "If you respond to this call, you can make a difference in the world." Some of us have lost that.
>
> — *Pastor Travis Collins*

A PROMPTING FROM GOD'S SPIRIT is what drew Travis Collins into the ministry twenty-five years ago. He believed then, and still does today, that the message of the gospel is a message that transforms lives. So in 2002 when Travis arrived in Richmond, Virginia, a city filled with historical sites tracing back to the early English settlers, and colonial buildings fortified with tall Corinthian columns, he was looking for a foundation for the church that was more than an architectural style. He wanted to know if Bon Air Baptist Church, the church calling him to be their senior pastor, shared his passion — God's work of transforming lives.

To understand the depth of Travis's passion, it helps to understand his family legacy. His story begins back in the early 1950s. Tent revivals were a regular part of religious life, especially in the South, and a church in Anniston, Alabama, felt that it was time for their city to experience revival. They erected a tent in an empty lot, scattered some sawdust on the dirt floor, and set up some chairs. Every evening for a week, a hellfire-and-brimstone preacher gave a rousing message for the tent meetings.

In that town was a man named JD who had been living a very rough life. JD was not the sort of guy you'd expect to see in church on Sunday morning. He was divorced from his first wife, and had no money and few prospects for employment. Eventually he found himself in Anniston, Alabama, and married again, but he was still far from the type of person most churches would welcome. A coworker invited JD to attend the revival meeting, and he agreed to go. As he listened to the preacher and his message, he reflected on his life. For the first time, he felt the stirring of hope, and after several revivall meetings, he had an unexpected and unusual experience that changed his life. His heart was changed and he met Jesus Christ. It was a moment that not only changed his life; it profoundly affected the life of his son, Travis.

Travis is quick to admit that he doesn't know where he would be today "if someone hadn't broken out of the mold and held that revival. And so I am interested in creating 'tent revivals,' not in the literal sense but in the sense that there are people like JD, my dad, that the average church might not have an interest in pursuing. And there are people like my dad who would not likely come to the average church either. I am quite certain that my dad would never have walked into the 'normal' church setting."

As a candidate for the position of senior pastor at Bon Air Baptist Church, Travis had one question: Would the church be willing to break out of the mold and be the kind of church that his dad had needed and found? Travis got connected with a couple on the leadership team of Bon Air who had started a different kind of ministry called NorthStar Community. As Travis talked with Pete and Teresa McBean (Teresa is one of the coauthors of this book), he realized that the people at Bon Air were indeed willing to do some creative and even risky things to see real life transformation. Travis listened to stories of lives that had been touched, redeemed, and transformed through this ministry, and he realized that he had found what he had been seeking — a "tent revival kind of church." In 2002 he became the senior pastor.

Bon Air has long been characterized as an externally focused, mission-minded church. The church had planted two new churches, was offering multiple services, was regularly sending teams of people out on mission trips, and had a clear emphasis on outreach to the community. But planting a recovery community was a different kind of move for them. When Travis first arrived at Bon Air, the North-Star initiative was three years old and was meeting at an elementary school not far from the church. They had no paid staff and were led by a team of volunteers.

NorthStar, as a recovery ministry, was reaching out to a nontraditional audience — people, like Travis's dad, who wouldn't be comfortable walking into a more traditional church setting. The church was lay led and passion driven. It had echoes of what Matthew's house must have felt like to the disenfranchised in Matthew 9:10 – 11: "While Jesus was having dinner at Matthew's house, many tax collectors and 'sinners' came and ate with him and his disciples. When the Pharisees saw this, they asked his disciples, 'Why does your teacher eat with tax collectors and "sinners"?'"

NorthStar was a place where people with real needs could feel welcome and have a chance to encounter Jesus.

Planting Churches

When I (Liz) first visited the city of Richmond to meet the staff of Bon Air Baptist Church, I thought, "The last thing the Richmond area needs is another church! There is hardly a corner without a church building of one denomination or another." I saw small chapels just a few blocks from larger stately churches. I saw churches with tall white steeples and several church buildings that looked to be several hundred years old. As I drove through the area, I noticed church after church after church, and I wondered, "Why plant a church in an area where there are already so many churches for people to attend?"

It's certainly a good question to ask, but I was forgetting that church buildings don't always indicate the presence of effective outreach. I quickly learned that the leaders of Bon Air were asking a very different question: "What groups of people are not currently being reached through existing churches?" The answer to *this* question was what had propelled them to plant their first two churches in different geographic parts of the city, places that still needed to experience the presence and power of Jesus and his followers.

While geography helps inform church planting, so does demography, profiling the people who live in a specific area. Demography asks a different question. It asks, Who are the people with unique needs or dreams, dispersed throughout the geography of the city, whom no one cares about? Who would never be loved and cared for through an existing church? And what can we do to reach those people? What the Richmond area did not need was another structure. But what it did need was a sacred space that transformed lives, a Matthew's house where broken people were not just welcomed but actually wanted. NorthStar was the answer to that question, a ministry designed to reach the unreached.

Messy but Transformational

From those early days in 1999, I (Teresa) was part of the leadership team of NorthStar. We rented a school cafeteria and set up chairs on the outside chance that someone might show up. This has always been a ministry that is difficult to define. It isn't neat and tidy. It's often messy and unpredictable. Our approach to church doesn't follow much of the conventional wisdom about how a church should be started or run. We set up shop as an ad hoc multisite church plant of Bon Air Baptist Church before we even knew what multisite church meant. Most of the principles that guide churches with multiple sites (one church, multiple campuses) hadn't been written when NorthStar was established, so we weren't operating with a clear set of guidelines or an established plan. More than a decade into the work, Bon Air and NorthStar continue to grapple with defining their relationship.

In fact, none of us at Bon Air really anticipated long-term viability. NorthStar never even made it into the church budget. Today this history is reflected in NorthStar's being both a ministry of Bon Air and a separate nonprofit organization — one completely funded by the people who attend. We considered the church something of a pilot project, a perspective that freed us to think outside the box of standard operating procedures. We didn't ask, "What will happen if we do this?" We asked, "What will happen if we don't?" We also believed that if we became too focused on thinking about things like infrastructure, models, programs, or standardizing our operational procedures, we might lose sight of what we did not know, and there was a lot we didn't know! We had absolutely no confidence in our system, but we had great anticipation as we trusted God's leadership and guidance.

In other words, we were students, learners on a quest for understanding. And we were willing to learn from almost anyone. We asked ourselves, What can we learn from therapists, from treatment facilities, from those in academia? Why do some hopelessly addicted end up sober while others end up in the morgue? What works and what doesn't? Who knows more than we do, and how can we learn from them? And who is sitting in the congregation each week who can teach us a thing or two or three about how to love others? We knew we had a lot to learn.

We lacked a road map, but we had a compass, a vision to facilitate transformation that became the "north star" to lead us forward in our journey. We united around a vision of changed lives, even as we wrestled with how it would all work organizationally. We also fielded several questions from people at Bon Air in the months leading up to our launch. "Who do you think will come when you advertise like this?" "Will anyone be willing to show up at a place that suggests that people with broken hearts, plaguing problems, addiction, and depression are welcomed, even encouraged to attend?" Even the ministry team honestly wondered who would come. We hoped for maybe ten people. Twenty would exceed all our expectations. We planned, prayed, prepared, and we waited.

At our first Sunday morning gathering, more than two hundred people poured through the doors of Bon Air Elementary School, an attendance buoyed by enthusiastic supporters from Bon Air Baptist Church! We pulled out additional chairs from nooks and crannies of the school cafeteria. Though our opening week numbers settled down to a more manageable eighty-five to one hundred after several weeks, the initial response was overwhelming. Because it was so unexpected, the influx of people at our opening sparked even more questions from the church. "What will you do now?" "After a few weeks, are you going to invite them to come to Bon Air Baptist?" "When will you guys stop meeting at the school and come back to regular church?" The response of our team was a sincere, "We don't know."

After several months of meeting, the NorthStar leadership team decided to host a picnic and listen to those attending this new ministry. We kept the meeting simple. Everyone interested in participating brought a bag lunch and planned to meet in the schoolyard after the Sunday service. The more organized in the group remembered to bring lawn chairs; the rest of us made do by sitting on the spotty patches of grass. Then the leadership team asked for feedback and any direction people had for the future. Consensus was quickly reached — something good was happening because God was at work, and the project should continue. The last comment voiced by one of the least vocal regulars at NorthStar still rings in my ears today: "I think that if Jesus were to come back to earth, this is the kind of church he'd attend."

When a church takes a leap of faith, especially an established church with a track record of making careful and wise decisions, they clearly hope that the leaders of the new venture know what they are doing! Although the particulars of how to operate caused organizational heartburn, no one could deny the tug of excitement as the church, the launch team, and the new members of NorthStar Community began to whisper in unison, "This might be a God thing." The "new thing" had become a "God thing." Encouraged by the response of the hatchling community, the NorthStar team rolled up their sleeves and got to work.

Living outside the Box

In the gospel of Mark, chapter 2, Jesus taught his followers a wise lesson regarding the process of change, using the illustration of wine and wineskins: "No one pours new wine into old wineskins. If he does, the wine will burst the skins, and both the wine and the wineskins will be ruined. No, he pours new wine into new wineskins" (v. 22).

Jesus and his followers knew that you can never pour new wine into old wineskins; the wine will ferment and expand, and the old, inflexible wineskins will stretch and break. Along with the spiritual implications of his teaching, there is also a practical lesson in change management here. As good as the old wineskins might be, as useful as they might have been in the past, and as good as the new wine might be, mixing them inevitably ruins both of them. This is why new wine must be poured into new animal skins, skins that are more flexible and able to expand as the wine ferments. Over time, wineskins lose their flexibility.

In our case, the pursuit of broken people in our community was the new wine given us. And since it was new, it required a new wineskin, a new structure for doing ministry. If recovery ministry was the new wine, NorthStar Community was the new wineskin. The leadership team of NorthStar Community knew that they would have to offer a new thing if they were going to reach out to families and offer a faith-based, love-based, and hope-based setting for those struggling with substance abuse.

The start-up nature of the recovery ministry pilot project meant that decisions regarding people and programs were being made and changed all the time, right up to launch time. One of those last-minute choices was asking me to take the lead in giving the message during the weekly celebration services at NorthStar. In my faith tradition and theological background, this was an unusual choice on many levels. I was (and still am) a woman who had no seminary training, and I was being asked to deliver a sermon on a Sunday morning in a Southern Baptist church. This, obviously, did not go unnoticed. While not everyone agreed with the selection, several leaders cleared the way so that the decision stood and the rest of the church extended grace, even if they disagreed. From my perspective, I+ it wasn't really my gender or the lack of seminary credentials that was was problematic. At a personal level, I lay awake at night wondering how the I could hope to speak with any clarity to a desperate crowd of people luck who were seeking answers to their plaguing problems. of

I relied heavily on the recovery community to help me craft a following

Biblical

Principles.

message that might encourage and support those seeking help with their struggles. I spent hours each day talking with my colaborers, thinking through my words and illustrations, wondering how they might sound to a guy sitting in the third row with a hangover, or the parent who shows up trying to find some assistance for their teenager caught in the trap of substance abuse. As I met people and heard their stories, I found myself amazed at how God was bringing people to our church, people who had plenty of experience, strength, and hope to share with us. I asked for feedback far more often than I handed out advice. I listened and learned and soon discovered that the "us" and "them" thinking was nothing more than an illusion. I recognized that all of us were in this stew pot together, asking God to show us where we needed to change.

Think Like a Missionary

The launch of the church was centered on a core vision: faith-based recovery ministry. We eliminated any traditions that might turn off or turn away the antichurch crowd, the dechurched, or the unchurched. We didn't pass an offering basket, have an altar call, or even ask people to sign a new visitor's card. (I confess that this approach still causes anxiety for me. If numbers drop for a season — and they do — I get nervous. I have internal wiring, from decades of living within the confines of a traditional church model, that sometimes fires away, urging me to do what I've always seen done. Honestly, thinking like a missionary requires a lot of determination and huge doses of community feedback and support.)

Our gatherings focus on the people attending, not the leadership. In this, we hope to create a collaborative environment where everyone brings their particular experiences, strengths, and hopes to the table. We believe that "the resources are in the harvest" and that God will provide the leadership and resources from inside the new community.

One of the key ministry start-up leaders was Bugsy King. Bugsy and his wife, Susan, had joined Bon Air Baptist years ago, as part of a treatment plan that was developed when Bugsy sought help for his addiction issues. Part of Bugsy's treatment plan included attending

ninety Alcoholics Anonymous meetings in ninety days and intro-
ducing a spiritual component to his life. Susan was advised to find
a support group and work on her codependency issues and to seek
spiritual support. Bugsy and Susan followed through on these suggestions and attended their respective meetings while visiting Bon
Air as part of their spiritual quest. They became active members
of the church and gradually revealed their story to trusted friends
within their new church home.

When it came time for the church to evaluate and design recovery curricula and processes, the staff naturally turned to Bugsy and
Susan King to lead this effort. Initially the team chose Celebrate
Recovery as a vehicle for launching a recovery ministry within the
church. As the ministry grew, the team decided to leverage the excellent reputation and trust of AA's twelve-step program by developing
a curriculum that used Christ-centered twelve-step material[22] as a
foundation for all their teaching and support group experiences.

Although some of the traditional AA groups within the area
regarded this faith-based recovery initiative at first with suspicion,
the respect that NorthStar had for AA's efforts soon allayed the fears
of most hardcore AAers. Because of a common AA language and
a common approach to recovery (using concepts like sponsorship,
anonymity, and solutions-focused support groups), NorthStar benefits from the experience of those brought up and educated within the
traditions of AA. Many of them have now joined NorthStar Community and are involved in the ministries of the church.

Most relatively small congregations would never consider starting
a television ministry, and certainly the idea wasn't even on our radar
until one of NorthStar's members identified a unique opportunity.
The local CBS affiliate had a thirty-minute spot available on Sunday
mornings for religious broadcasting. While Bon Air's senior pastor,
Travis Collins, felt that the Richmond area needed another traditional Sunday message like a mule needs a spinning wheel (that is,
they didn't need one), the thought of reaching people no one else was
reaching through traditional church appealed to him. Why not offer
a Christ-centered, twelve-step recovery message through television,
instead of the traditional church sermon? There were certainly lots of
families suffering in isolation and silence, trying to deal with hidden

addictions and problems. Could we get into their homes through their TVs? It was in answering this question that Bon Air's television ministry was launched with a commitment to send hope to hurting families no one else was reaching.

Weekly television broadcasts soon produced another unexpected opportunity. Grandmothers and sisters, moms and dads started writing in to the program, asking for help. Many of them had relatives sitting in jail cells. All of them believed that substance abuse was part of the reason for their incarceration, and they were right.

Several volunteers at NorthStar reached out to those in prison. A team of teachers and writers worked on the Christ-centered twelve-step materials that were being used in the support groups, and produced a correspondence course. Today these materials are being used throughout the Virginia prison system in collaboration with Bon Air's thriving prison ministry. In partnership with Prison Fellowship Ministry and the Virginia Department of Corrections, two prisons in the state offer a weekly twelve-step recovery meeting as one component of a pilot project designed to help inmates prepare for transition back into the community. Recently the Virginia Department of Corrections asked for an expansion of these meetings into other prisons in the state. NorthStar Community and the Chaplain Services of Virginia are working to make recovery accessible in every prison and jail for every qualified candidate in need of these services throughout Virginia.

More Is Not Always Better

In traditional ministries, increased numbers are one obvious sign of success. And as NorthStar grew numerically, some assumed that this was a big win for us. But we knew that simple numeric growth wasn't necessarily good news for the people attending. Effective life change is not always easy in a large group. More is not always better. In an effort to keep the large group celebration services small enough for dialogue and questions between the audience and their minister, NorthStar added a second recovery-based service on Saturday evenings, returning to our roots at Bon Air to plant this new community. Following that, we planted two additional NorthStar

Community fellowships in churches located on the outskirts of Richmond. Other smaller fellowships are also being planned, groups that can retain the smaller size that allows for optimal personal and spiritual growth through the recovery process.

Collaborate to Multiply Your Impact

One of the guiding Scriptures at NorthStar comes from the wisdom of Solomon: "It's better to have a partner than go it alone. Share the work, share the wealth. And if one falls down, the other helps, but if there's no one to help, tough! Two in a bed warm each other. Alone, you shiver all night. By yourself you're unprotected. With a friend you can face the worst. Can you round up a third? A three-stranded rope isn't easily snapped" (Eccl. 4:9 – 12 MSG).

NorthStar Community is eager to learn from and work with like-hearted people. We look for other organizations in the community that share a common passion for healing people and changing lives. One such partnership is with The Healing Place, a local treatment facility that serves homeless addicted men in the city of Richmond. Partnering together, we each benefit from the strengths of the other. The Healing Place also uses a traditional twelve-step model for recovery based on AA's model. To meet some of the spiritual needs of those in the recovery process, NorthStar sends two buses every Sunday to The Healing Place to transport those looking for a place to worship to NorthStar Community's suburban Bon Air location. Because NorthStar has embraced the cause of this treatment center, we regularly provide them with financial support and run a recovery meeting at the facility one night a week.

One of my favorite experiences on a Sunday morning is grabbing a cup of coffee and watching as thirty or so homeless guys study God's Word with a bunch of suburbanite men. And this isn't a one-way conversation either. They are learning from each other. Though these men differ in their ethnicity, socioeconomic status, and even fashion sense (my husband is often teased about his preppy style), they unite and are drawn together by the belief that only God can save them. They bond as they share their experience of struggling with sin and searching for God in the midst of deep personal shame. While many pastors struggle to find ways to increase diversity and bring in new visitors, this is happening naturally in our church community.

One Size Doesn't Fit All

One time we had a guy in our NorthStar community who was repeatedly relapsing into his old habits and ways. Finally his wife did something different — and a bit unexpected! She kicked him out. He ended up at the local shelter. It was a joy for our church community to watch as the restoration process unfolded. None of it was quick or easy. He found himself living out of the house much longer than he liked, but his recovery might have been sidetracked if he had been granted a return too soon. There was a day when this man couldn't walk into a bank and receive service; today he owns his own home, has a job he loves, and works tirelessly with other guys who are searching for a way back home, just as he once was. Admittedly, he still has bad days. But now he has a community that is committed to him and holds him accountable through encouragement and ongoing support.

Another man, now part of our NorthStar community, had relapsed so frequently that eventually the treatment facilities began to refuse him service, even though he was a paying customer! The last halfway house he visited sent him home with a suggestion that he try something different and get reconnected with his spiritual community. They weren't trying to encourage him; they suggested he find a church because he was going to need someone to bury him soon! Through all this, his wife never left his side.

Eventually he found a specialist in addiction who prescribed a blend of medications that was effective in helping to eradicate some of his cravings. Many of the people in his recovery support system shook their heads at him in disgust. After all, they had gotten sober without the help of pharmacology and fancy drugs. Wasn't he just cheating the system, taking a shortcut? Despite their criticisms, he was able to truly benefit from the research of doctors like Dr. Hal Urschel[23] and avail himself of the latest treatment in addiction. Part of our ongoing challenge is to spread the message that there are effective medical interventions available today, advances that were not even possible when Bill W. first founded Alcoholics Anonymous.

Today this couple, Mike and Donna Thompson, are managing the NorthStar prison ministry program, a ministry that brings hope to thousands of addicts locked up and dealing with their own addictions. Mike still takes the meds as they are prescribed by his psychiatrist, a doctor who specializes in the treatment of addiction. Mike works a twelve-step program, and he faithfully attends NorthStar Community. Through it all, his wife, Donna, never kicked him out or wavered in her support. He has enjoyed years of sobriety. Needless to say, there are no immediate plans for his funeral!

These are the stories of just two couples from our church. Each followed a different path to healing, yet both found freedom from impossibly powerful addictions — long-term, intractable addictions. Perhaps the most beautiful part of these two stories is not just that these couples found freedom but also that they were both involved in a faith community that was willing to allow more than just one right approach to healing.

Success Is Learning from Failure

The NorthStar team discovered that effectiveness in ministry is the product of many inefficiencies and setbacks. Every failure is a learning experience that teaches the community what won't work. Failure is never viewed as a sign that God is not at work! The teachings and practice of Jesus lend credence to this approach. "A farmer went out to sow his seed. As he was scattering the seed, some fell along the path.... Some fell on rocky places.... Other seed fell among thorns.... Still other seed fell on good soil" (Mark 4:3 – 8).

Jesus, like the farmer, throws out the seed of the gospel indiscriminately, trusting God with the results of his preaching. He used neither military force (although he could have called angels to his side in a heartbeat and wiped out all opposition) nor miracle-working powers to accomplish his mission. Instead, he called people to respond to the Word of God, to repent and believe the good news. Jesus left the results of his ministry up to his Father and simply spoke the message to whoever would listen. The work of the kingdom of God is about sowing seeds — and leaving the results up to God.

Several years ago, two local churches initiated a conversation with me about the possibility of adding a recovery ministry program to their existing church. Each church formed a recovery ministry launch team and began doing some training. One church chose to worship on Sunday mornings, the other on Sunday evenings. They jointly attended a weekend workshop led by the NorthStar staff. Both churches worked diligently in preparing for their new ministry start-up. The senior pastors at both churches met with the NorthStar Community team and then with their own teams — fully supportive of the efforts to reach out into their communities through a recovery ministry.

On February 10, 2008, both churches kicked off their programs. One ministry survived, while the other did not. Today Craig Simpson continues to serve as pastor of NorthStar Community at Walnut Grove Baptist Church in Mechanicsville, Virginia. They average forty or so in attendance each Sunday morning and offer support groups for both men and women interested in finding solutions to their problems using the Christ-centered twelve-step materials.

As a ministry leader, I am grateful that these two experimental ministry start-ups occurred. I suppose if we had started only at Walnut Grove and experienced it as a success, we might have thought we really knew what we were doing. But the other start-up didn't take root, and that gives us appropriate reason to pause and marvel at the grace of God. I wholeheartedly believe that both churches had great potential, but I cannot state with confidence why one flourished and the other never really gained traction.

We're learning to apply to ourselves what we are learning from those we are seeking to help. I've watched brave men and women willingly acknowledge their powerlessness over addictions, unchecked codependency, and a whole host of other issues. They know firsthand that the road to recovery is not a straight path, yet they keep walking. They've learned that failure isn't fatal, nor is success always final. We, like them, are also on a journey. I've learned that just because something we try doesn't work, that's not the same thing as saying it failed. I've learned to enjoy the freedom that comes from no longer having to evaluate everything I do in terms of success or failure. In keeping with the way Jesus taught us to sow seeds, we try faithfully to sow his message and ministry wherever we can, and leave the results up to God.

People in recovery learn how to cope with adversity. Tom and Terrie Cook, the leaders of the recovery ministry that did not launch, validate this. Terrie describes the process of dealing with their failure to launch: "Slowly and surely, I did what I had learned. I paused to prepare, I prayed and listened, I kept my options open, I got out of my own way and looked at everything as a lesson instead of a defeat," she says. Husband Tom adds to Terrie's account. "Not too long after this, we went to NorthStar at Bon Air. We were talking with Pete McBean about our move, and he said it best: 'Sometimes you have to find where God is working and go there.'"

Today Tom and Terrie serve in a different way by participating in the prison ministry at NorthStar and at the new NorthStar Community at Walnut Grove. "We eventually went to visit NorthStar at Walnut Grove. Admittedly, it was difficult to do so. We have been welcomed and are part of the team. Not being leaders takes the pressure off. The community is growing. The most important thing to come of this is that it has brought us closer as a couple. We help others, others help us. It's great. I really feel like we are where God wants us to be."

At NorthStar, individuals as well as teams take risks because they don't worry about whether something will succeed. Pastor Travis Collins believes that reaching out through the vehicle of a recovery ministry not only provides an opportunity to pitch tents for revival but also brings healing and encouragement to pastors. "What a pastor does is very hard," he said. "I think that pastors are hurting because doing church is more complicated than ever, and the idea of taking on one more thing is daunting. But beginning to think along these lines may actually save your ministry. It could give you a new sense of purpose. It could save you from the 'administrivia' that is killing you, sucking the life out of you.

"This ministry is about transformation, and you see it here in a dramatic way. It gets you back in touch with why you got into this in the first place. It can rekindle your passion for ministry. There is a broad segment of the population that needs Jesus, and you are never going to engage them without providing a doorway."

Recovery ministry can be that doorway.

Questions for Reflection and Discussion

1. There was a day when tent revivals "broke the mold." In some ways, recovery ministry also breaks a mold. In what ways is your ministry breaking a mold to reach people who would never set foot in a church — your church?

2. In church, we have various means of measuring. We measure attendance numbers and amounts of offering. We measure how many people are in small groups and Sunday school classes. How do we measure transformation?

3. What if your church looked like Matthew's house (Matt. 9:10 – 11)? Describe what that would look like.

4. What will happen if your church doesn't have a ministry for recovery and healing?

chapter six

CRISIS IN A SMALL TOWN

Caveland Baptist Church

> The ministry of recovery is not just a passion of mine; it's personal. I am a pastor, and we have a son in jail right now because he can't quit using drugs.
>
> —*Pastor Chad Hunt*

"GOD IS GOING TO GIVE YOU A UNIQUE MINISTRY."

It was the second night of the revival meetings, and after he had shared his evening message with the crowd of people gathered that night, the revival preacher walked directly up to Chad, indicating that he needed to speak with him and his wife. Chad Hunt had never met the man before, and he wasn't quite sure what he wanted.

As they talked, the preacher suddenly looked directly into Chad's eyes and in a solemn voice spoke these words to him: "God is going to give you a unique ministry. Not every church is going to accept it, but you will be called to do it." The preacher was clear that he did not know all of the details of what he was saying, but he had an unshakable sense from God that Chad was going to do something in the future that would have a large impact on the church.

Chad had no idea what he was talking about.

At the time, Chad had been a pastor for only six months. He wasn't all that sure how to respond to what he had been told. In general, Baptists are somewhat skeptical about prophetic utterances, but still, Chad kept the words in the back of his mind. As years passed and Chad pastored and led the church, the words of that night would come to mind from time to time. He often wondered if they would ever mean anything. Eventually, after thirteen years of ministry in the church, a unique and innovative recovery ministry called Addiction Deliverance Outreach (ADO) was birthed through Chad's leadership, and he witnessed the fulfillment of God's promise to him that night long ago.

Where Everybody Knows Your Name

Caveland Baptist Church is located in Cave City, Kentucky. Cave City is a small town of about two thousand residents that sits about thirty miles northeast of Bowling Green. Cave City, as you might guess, is known for its multitude of caves. Tourists and spelunkers come from all over the world to tour or explore the Cave Spring Caverns, Lost River Caves, Mammoth Cave, or Outlaw Cave. Caveland Church boasts a weekend worship attendance of five hundred, a rather large congregation for a small town like Cave City — 25 percent of the town's population.

Caveland Church was started in 1994 with thirty-three members meeting in a tobacco barn, and Sammy Hunt, Chad's father, was the first pastor of the church. In 1995, Caveland Church leased a vacant church building, and membership grew to one hundred. Then, in 2000, Pastor Sammy Hunt was called to a new church, and Chad, who had been working as the youth pastor, was selected to take the position as senior pastor.

Growing up in a small town has many advantages. One advantage is that everyone knows you. But small towns also have some disadvantages, and one disadvantage is that everyone knows you! Chad grew up a preacher's kid, and he quickly learned that his personal business became everyone's business. In his teen years, when he went through a stage of rebelliousness, he became the talk of the town. He drank too much, smoked pot, and partied hard, living as a prodigal son for several years before returning home to the church that had raised him. Chad's reputation as a bad boy probably exceeded the reality of his exploits, but it all worked in his favor after the Lord turned his life around. When he was a youth pastor, parents in the town, knowing his reputation, brought their rebellious kids to him in the hope that he could help them navigate their own difficulties. "We know where you've come from. We know you understand what our kids are going through, and we think you can help us," parents would say to him. From the earliest days of Chad's ministry as a youth pastor, people trusted him with their family secrets and problems as they struggled through crisis situations. Soon the nature of these problems began to take on epic proportions.

Nothing to Say

One day as Chad was driving home after a particularly long day at the church office, he received a phone call from a woman who regularly attended Caveland. She sounded desperate and panicked. Apparently, there was something wrong with her husband. Chad could hear the fear in her voice, and he knew it was serious, so he drove to his home, picked up his wife, and together they tried to assess what caused the distressed woman to react with such alarm. Her husband seemed like a clean-cut, well-educated man, and he always brought his family to the Sunday services. But when they arrived at the home, they were greeted by the wife — visibly shaken and frightened — and her equally frightened children. The wife cried out to them, "He's on a crack binge again."

What? Crack binge? Again? Chad had no idea what she was talking about at first. As the story spilled from her lips, they learned that her husband had taken all of their money, even selling their personal computer, to get more of this powerful drug. Chad was astonished and tried hard to believe what the woman was telling him. It seemed impossible that *this man* could be a crackhead! He was obviously a hardworking, churchgoing, salt-of-the-earth family man. He even shouted amen during the service! "I realized then that I did not know what to say to them," Chad admits. "I tried to encourage them, and I prayed for them, but I really had nothing to offer them that could directly address their problem."

This was the first indication to Chad that there was a rapidly growing problem with drug abuse in his town, and not only in the town of Cave City but also right in his church! The problem was exacerbated by the influx and availability of methamphetamines in the form of crack. Even though crack had been around since the 1980s, it quickly became epidemic around 2000, especially in small towns all around the country, towns just like Chad's. Soon meth addiction and the resulting behaviors began to take over the life of the town. Chad said, "I began to hear stories about children being left at home alone for days at a time—neglected and abused. About moms and dads running off and abandoning their families. People were being incarcerated. Individuals who were at one time outstanding, functioning citizens had gotten strung up on meth, their lives destroyed. It broke my heart. And what was even stranger was that so many of these people began showing up at my church. I finally said to God in desperation, 'You keep sending me all of these people with their addictions, and I don't know what to do to help them.'"

Parents came to Chad, begging him to help their children. People walked into his office desperate and looking for answers, not moral platitudes. Chad felt powerless. Attempting to give reassurance that things would be okay felt hollow and empty. "I prayed for them, preached at them, and told them to come to church. Some were saved, but having their names written in the Book of Life didn't automatically fix the addiction. They still had the problem, the addiction, the habit. The only difference was that they were now saved people with addictions," he said. Chad found himself having to officiate funerals for kids in their teens, as well as men and women in their sixties and seventies, who had lost their lives to this powerful addiction.

Breakthrough—a Dream Fulfilled

Chad became heavily burdened for the people in his church and in his community. He looked to God to give him direction. He got down on his knees and sought the Lord for answers. And God gave him three words: addiction, deliverance, and outreach. He wrote the words down and added a description after each word:

Addiction: their problem
Deliverance: God's work
Outreach: the church's responsibility

God had given him a rough draft of a rehabilitation ministry. The recovery curriculum that Chad developed was built around a simple four-step process: acceptance, education, accountability, and recovery. Each step had multiple sessions and was designed to work in a church setting (and across denominational lines). The process itself could be used in conjunction with other recovery efforts or serve as a stand-alone program. Chad's desire was to provide guidance for his church, as well as for anyone with a heart for helping the addicted. "The uniqueness of Addiction Delivery Outreach (ADO) was the provision of one-on-one mentorship. The person who was struggling and a counselor would meet weekly for one hour." Much as in the AA model of sponsorship, in the ADO program, the individual and their counselor would work through an ADO workbook together. Both the counselor and the individual would have separate, compatible workbooks to work through independently during the week, and then they would discuss them during their hour-long sessions. It was a flexible plan, and it proved to be highly effective as well.

Chad and his wife, Melissa, started counseling addicts and their families. Soon not just church members were seeking help; people from the community began to show up at the church as well. Meth cooks (who put together the chemicals that create crack) started coming to the church looking for help. In fact, some of the best meth cooks in the country started showing up and coming to Christ. Many began the long struggle of recovery through the ADO materials, and many of these same meth cooks, who had often been arrested and incarcerated, also began to experience transformation. They started going to the court dates with their friends who were still using drugs and asked the judge if he would allow their friends to go through the ADO program.

One day Chad got a call from a Barren County Court judge. "Am I speaking to Chad Hunt?" the judge asked him.

"Yes, sir, you are."

"What is the ABO program?"

"Well, I don't know what ABO is, but I do know about ADO."

"Well," said the judge, "all I know is that I keep having people come before me who have been incarcerated multiple times in the past and have now become self-appointed advocates for their friends who are up for sentencing. They keep talking about having their friends go through this ADO program, and I just want to know if this ADO is legit."

Chad shared the story of what had happened and how the program was run. Before the conversation ended, the judge asked one final question. "Is there any way we can use your program as an alternative option for recovery?"

"Yes, sir, you certainly may!" Chad said.

The unique ministry that had been promised to Chad thirteen years earlier was now being realized. God's promise had proven true.

Good News Travels Fast

In a town of two thousand, this type of decision quickly becomes front-page news. The news that the ADO program was an official option for men and women facing incarceration for drug offenses significantly raised the profile of the church. Soon the judge was "sentencing" people to attend church by giving them three options upon conviction: "You can go to jail, pay one thousand dollars a day for a recovery program, or go through the ADO program at Caveland Church."

Soon other pastors started calling Chad and asking for help as well. Chad and his staff began training leaders who were interested and passing along the ADO materials. (On the Barren County Correction Center website is a link that says, "Inmate Services: Introduction to ADO Program.")

Over time, Caveland Church developed a reputation as a place where people could come to find acceptance and healing. Today at Caveland Church you will find people who have incredible stories to tell, people who are now free to tell them, and free from bondage to addiction. Kevin, for instance, was a crack addict and a crack cook. If you are not familiar with crack, it's hard to explain the addictive power of the drug. People will do things on crack they would never do when sober. They do things they wouldn't even be able to do when not under the influence of the drug. When the police showed up at Kevin's home for a domestic violence call, Kevin — high on crack — greeted the arresting officer by tossing him over the police car.

It wasn't the best way to welcome a guest, especially a police officer. After a tough battle involving several officers, Kevin finally was subdued and hauled off to jail. He had three charges against him: domestic violence, assaulting a police officer, and, after the police discovered the meth lab in his home, manufacturing illegal drugs.

After sitting in jail for several weeks and finally getting sober again, he realized how screwed up his life was and how much he needed help. He knew that he was helpless against the power of the drug, and he wanted to make some changes. People from Caveland Church visited Kevin in jail and led him to Christ. Obviously, becoming a Christian doesn't erase history. Kevin was still facing a fifteen-year sentence for his assault on the officer, so while he was out on bail, before his final sentencing, Kevin enrolled in the ADO program at Caveland Church. Slowly he began to experience the power of God changing his life.

Pastor Chad accompanied Kevin to court for his final sentencing. (There have been only two other people whom Chad has been willing to vouch for in court.) From the bench the judge looked at Chad, whom by now he knew quite well, and asked, "Chad, what do you think about Kevin? Has he changed?"

"Well, sir, if he is faking all this, he belongs in Hollywood," Chad replied.

That day, the judge made a life-changing decision for Kevin. He released him into the care of Chad and the ADO program. And since his release six years ago, Kevin has been living clean, free from drugs, and is now helping others connect to the ADO program. He also serves as the head usher at Caveland Church and is a key leader at the church. He owns his own trucking company, lives in a new home, and is married, with a son in college. He and his wife are now experiencing the healing that comes from an encounter with God's grace.

Everybody Hurts Sometimes

Although Chad and his wife had seen many lives transformed by God and had witnessed the reality of how God can work through miraculous transformation, they soon found themselves dealing with their own drama at home. Despite their best efforts, Chad's eldest son had become ensnared by the problem of substance abuse. The oldest of four children, Chad's son was a kind and compassionate young man who was never difficult or outwardly rebellious as a child. But when he turned sixteen, he began hanging out with some friends and smoking pot, which soon led to a hard-core addiction to meth. He was arrested several times and put in jail for a period of time. Chad and his wife still remember many nights when they returned home from church, quickly running to their son's room just to see if he was okay, if he was still alive. As they considered the terrifying consequences of the choices their son was making, they experienced many of the same fears that the families they had counseled had experienced. Their biggest fear was that they might lose him one day.

Eventually their son stopped using meth, but like many addicts, he moved on to yet another abusive relationship, this time with Loracet, a prescription drug that combines acetaminophen and hydrocodone, an opiate used to treat pain. It's a habit-forming drug that is closely linked to morphine. Today Chad's son is twenty-seven years old and is still serving time in prison for violating his probation after testing positive for Loracet. As of this writing, he is preparing to visit a long-term rehab center.

Despite these challenges, Chad remains hopeful. "We believe that God still has a plan for our son's life. We know that just because we see some people come to Christ and go through recovery, then go on to experience real life change, it doesn't mean it is going to happen that way for everyone. We know that sometimes God works through the wilderness experience and that some people also need medical intervention. God can use all sorts of ways. The thing that we have had to understand is that we need to take our hands off our son's life. We have felt the pressure to fix him. But the truth is that we have a son in jail right now, and it's because he can't quit using drugs." If even the pastor's son is not immune to the powerful lure of the growing drug culture in Cave City, it's a sobering reminder to each of us that the power of addiction can affect anyone, regardless of name or reputation.

Close to Home

As I (Liz) interviewed pastors and leaders around the nation, many of them took me aside and shared with me stories about their family members. They talked about a teenager who was rebelling against the church and had turned his or her back on the faith or was engaged in some type of sexual sin. They described the heartbreak of discovering that one of their children was taking drugs. Some of the leaders talked about the pain they were feeling because a family member was battling a full-blown addiction. One pastor spoke of the relief he had knowing that both of his kids were now finally in rehab getting the help they needed. This man's daughter was at an eating disorder clinic in Arizona, and his son had just entered an in-patient drug rehab facility in California. I remember an interview I did with a pastor in Arizona who talked about trying to teach parents whose kids were going through a crisis that they couldn't "put the keys to their happiness into the hands of their children." This was more than good advice or a moral platitude. She herself had walked through the experience after her eighteen-year-old son was sent to prison for dealing cocaine.

As Chad's story and the work of God at Caveland Church teach us, being a pastor or a leader in the church does not exempt your family from hardship and suffering. While we may wish that those who "do things God's way" would always find blessing and experience healthy family dynamics, we know that life doesn't always work that way. For leaders who have a family member in crisis, struggling with addiction or substance abuse, the unspoken expectations that we place on church leaders can make the burden they carry feel even more heavy and difficult. Often, pastors' families are closely scrutinized by the congregation, and those who are watching may be looking for explanations. Pastors may hear people say to them, "If you are so godly, how come your family is having this kind of problem?" Congregants can quickly turn into Job's friends, wrongly concluding that there must be a direct, parental cause behind a child's or close family member's sin and moral failure.

An Unchanging Word

When Chad became the senior pastor at Caveland Church, he brought with him a reputation he had earned as a rebellious young man. When you live in a small town like Cave City, there are few secrets. But when his son began to have problems, well ... that was a whole new challenge. How does a pastor or a Christian who has attempted to live a life of faith respond when their family is in crisis? Chad offers this counsel: "What do we do? We press on. We move forward, teaching the truth, regardless of whether that truth seems like it is manifested in our personal lives. The reality is, the Word of God is still true regardless of what happens in our personal lives. The apostle Paul spoke with great conviction from a jail cell about freedom and liberty; there is irony in ministry."

Chad has had to listen to the comments and criticisms. He has had to walk through the dark nights of fear and disappointment. But as he reflects on all this, there is one thing that he keeps in mind: life is made up of seasons. The seasons of life, just like those we experience in nature, have a beginning and they have an end. Chad tries to take a broader perspective on his suffering and struggle. Sometimes we go through good seasons, and sometimes we go through bad seasons, and it's in the midst of the most difficult seasons when we tend to succumb to the lie that things will never get better, that they will never end. But Chad remembers that the bad seasons are still used by God to build "persistence and vigor" into the lives of his people. He remembers a story that often encourages him when things look bleak and his hope fails: "One year, I decided to plant a watermelon patch. I called my grandfather, a longtime Kentucky farmer, for advice. He told me to make little hills out of the dirt and drop the seeds into each mound. So I formed small hills and planted the seeds. The seeds sprouted and grew beautiful little plants.

"However, we hit about two weeks with no rain, and the leaves began to wilt. I called my grandfather and asked him how much water I should pour on the wilting plants. He said, 'None, Chad. When it's dry, the roots will go deeper into the ground, searching for water. The deeper the roots go, the cooler the water will be, which in turn will make your watermelons all the sweeter.'"

Chad and his wife have watched their son walk through the devastation of drug addiction. They have done their best to help him. At times, they have likely overwatered his life in eager attempts to save their son, whose life seemed to be wilting before their eyes. But over time they have come to accept an important truth: they cannot fix him or change him. That kind of change and lasting transformation has to be done in his heart, and it's a work that only God can do. Instead, they remind themselves that in this season of their son's life, God is still at work and may be doing things they cannot see, in both their son's life and their own lives.

Seasons change. They have a beginning, and they have an end.

Brokenness Is a Bridge

Chad and his wife, Melissa, also have had to accept that they will never have the picture-perfect family some pastors do. At one point, they realized they had a decision to make. They could continue to hide what was going on, a complex and difficult task, or they could acknowledge what was happening and openly admit that they had family problems. Pretending that nothing is going on when there is a glaring problem in his life makes a pastor seem naive, like he is living in denial, or worse, that he is disingenuous and deceptive. While Chad celebrates the good stories, the families in which the daughter becomes a choir director and the son becomes a youth pastor, he knows that is not his story. Instead, he has something to offer that others may not — a different way to minister. "When a mother comes to church in fear with tears running down her cheeks because of her addicted daughter, she is not looking for a sermon. She is looking for someone who has been there, or still is, and is surviving. She is looking for someone who can humbly say, 'I know how you feel,' and mean it." Chad admits that even though he has a degree in theology and Christian ministry, the best ministry tool is often his own experience as a father. Parents need to hear words of hope that address them where they live, and Chad's personal experience gives his words a ring of authenticity. He's been there.

Questions for Reflection and Discussion

1. Where can pastors and lay leaders in your community go to find support and encouragement without fear of judgment?

2. When a pastor comes clean about his own problems, what are the benefits of that kind of authenticity for the congregation? What are the risks?

3. If your pastor's family was experiencing a major crisis, how do you think your church would respond?

4. What resources does your church have for families in distress?

chapter seven

THE PEOPLE EVERY CHURCH WANTS

Grace United Methodist Church

> Lord, send us the people nobody else wants or sees.
> — *Pastor Jorge Acevedo*

JORGE ACEVEDO HAS BEEN THE LEAD PASTOR of Grace United Methodist Church, a multisite congregation in Cape Coral, Florida, since 1996. When I (Liz) first arrived at Grace Church to interview Jorge (pronounced "George"), I noticed that the church was having some construction work done to mend damage that had occurred during the recent hurricane season. But as I entered Jorge's office, I was greeted with a warm and boisterous welcome that immediately put me at ease. Jorge is a man with little pretense — and a huge capacity for caring.

Over the past few years, Grace Church has grown into a church of three campuses with more than 2,600 people attending their weekend services. In addition, more than eight hundred people engage in the recovery ministries offered by the church at various locations scattered around Cape Coral.

A City of Contradictions

Located on the southwest coast of Florida, the city of Cape Coral is mostly known for its beaches, mild climate, and great fishing. It's a predominately white, working-class community that is also home to a growing Latino population. In addition to the sandy beaches, Cape Coral has another distinguishing feature. Shortly after President Obama was elected, he made a point of visiting some of the nation's most economically distressed cities, cities with the highest unemployment and the largest number of home foreclosures in 2009.

Cape Coral was on the president's list.

In many ways, Cape Coral is a city of contradictions. Resplendent with an intrinsic natural beauty and historic charm, it's also a town rife with financial distress and shocking crime statistics — almost triple the national average in most categories. So when Jorge Acevedo began his work as a pastor at Grace Church, he knew that he was coming to a city with great needs. On the morning of his first sermon as a new pastor, Jorge knelt in his office and prayed a heartfelt prayer: "Lord, send us the people nobody else wants or sees." At the time, Jorge had no idea just how seriously God would honor that prayer. But the story of Grace Church is the story of an answered prayer. Since that day, God has been at work for nearly fifteen years as alcoholics, drug addicts, codependents, and angry and hurting people have poured into Grace Church. The people nobody wants have found a place to belong — and experience God's healing.

You Attract Who You Are

During my time with Pastor Jorge, we talked extensively about the nature of recovery ministry and the way his church has tried to aid people as they walk through the process of recovery and healing. When I asked him a question, Jorge pensively paused and reflected before answering: "The nuts and bolts of recovery ministry are not what make it work. What makes it work are the unspoken assumptions. They are the theological underpinnings foundational to the ministry — the DNA that serves as the values or reasons behind the ministry. It comes down to a deeply held, organic conviction that recovery ministry is all about how much we value people."

Jorge believes you attract who you are, not who you want to be. Since Jorge himself comes from a messy and dysfunctional family (extending back several generations), it is no surprise to him that the church he pastors is filled with other "messed-up people." Jorge was born in Puerto Rico and is quite proud of his cultural heritage and ethnic background. Yet tied into the richness of his heritage were some unhealthy beliefs and expectations. Jorge remembers his grandfather once telling him that he would be not considered a man until he had married a wife, fathered children, and had a couple of girlfriends on the side. Having been raised with this definition of manhood, Jorge soon began living out his own patterns of dysfunction and sin.

In fact, by the time Jorge was a senior in high school, he was already well on his way to becoming an alcoholic. Though he was making good grades in school, his life was a mess. By God's grace, Jorge came to Christ during those rough high school years, got involved with a good church, and began doing all the right things. But he was still hiding many secrets. "I would drink on the weekends and repent on Monday. I was saved and miserable. . . . I just kept trying to 'pray things away.'" After graduating from high school, Jorge married his high school sweetheart and sensed a call into full-time ministry. Though the call was authentic and powerful, Jorge admits that he was still an angry "dry drunk" who exhibited all the characteristics of an alcoholic — without the alcohol. "I was saved, but my life did not reflect that fact in many ways. I was verbally abusive to my wife and neglectful. All this stemmed back to the roots of an addiction that I had never properly dealt with," admits Jorge.

During the ordination process, his denomination required that he undergo stringent psychological evaluations. As Jorge went through the testing, his addiction became very clear to him and the board. He began to see a counselor who had the wisdom to walk Jorge down a path of recovery from his damaged past. But even though he began to see changes in his life, it was not until his brother began attending Alcoholics Anonymous and receiving treatment for his addictions that Jorge became familiar with the ministry of recovery. Jorge began to explore the biblical principles on which AA was founded, and he realized that this was an area where people needed help and healing.

A Timely Prayer

"Send us the people no one else sees or wants."

When Jorge first heard that prayer uttered by a pastor at a church he was visiting, he was struck by the welcome and the generous love behind the request. Still, as he glanced around the sanctuary of the church that day, he couldn't overlook the fact that everyone appeared to have been stamped out of the same mold. The seats were mostly occupied by successful white Americans. And to Jorge's eyes, they certainly didn't look like the people no one else saw or wanted. Still, he knew that it was a good prayer, and he made a mental note to remember it, because it was a prayer that clearly captured God's heart for hurting and marginalized people. Years later, as Jorge was preparing to give his first sermon to a half-empty church, he found himself down on his knees crying out to God and praying that very same prayer: "Lord, send us the people nobody else wants or sees." He wanted to begin his ministry as a pastor by leading a church that would welcome the people no one else wanted, and though he had no idea how his plea would be answered, he knew that he was desperate for God to show up.

For the first several years, there were no immediate, noticeable changes. Jorge faithfully served as the pastor at Grace Church, concentrating his energy on giving people a vision for reaching out beyond the walls of the church building. Grace was a church that needed to learn how to "turn the arrows from pointing inside, toward their own lives, back to pointing out toward others." As more and more people embraced the externally focused vision that Jorge was sharing, attendance grew. Within a couple of years, they had more than doubled in size, with more than one thousand people attending services each week. In addition, the church had a growing ministry to the community. Most pastors would have considered Jorge's work a success, but there was something that still bothered Jorge, despite the great success and growth. Although many people were coming to know Jesus Christ, Jorge could also see that many were still struggling with their sins and addictions. "I could see that they were delivered from the hell they were headed to ... but not from the hell they were living in." Jorge observed that many of his parishioners were doing their best to live the Christian life, yet they were still burdened by their wounds, addictions, and an assortment of other issues that sabotaged their best efforts to seek after God. "I do not buy into a theology that says we are always delivered from our afflictions, but I do believe Scripture teaches that we are in a process of recovery from the damage." For Jorge, the ministry of recovery is not just theology for messed-up people with problems and addictions; it's a theology for every one of us as we grow more and more into the image and likeness of Christ. "We all have an 'it,' " he says. "I know my 'it' revolves around control, power, and anger. But when I know what my 'it' is, it's a lot easier to say, 'Yes, that's my issue,' and to let Jesus work on it. But when people are unaware that they have issues, they can cause all sorts of wounds to others both in the church and outside the church."

Three Priorities

To make Grace Church a place where people could recover from the damage and pain in their lives, Jorge began with a reappraisal of three key areas: the people, the places, and the processes for recovery. Jorge found himself asking two questions: Are people at the heart of our ministry? Do we prioritize people over programs, personnel, and properties? He answered those questions by assessing the processes that were currently in place to help people take steps of healing. Jorge redefined the healing ministries of the church so that the intention was clear: to help people get well God's way. God's way of healing is the process the Bible calls sanctification, our growing freedom from the power of sin. "Many churches ... offer people Jesus the Healer without offering healing ministries. They are faithful to the evangelistic call to know Jesus as the forgiver, healer, and leader of their lives, but they stop short of helping the new relationship take root inside the battered life of the young Christ-follower. If we do not offer the places, the people, and the processes for people to heal, we are offering only half of the gospel. We offer them only the Jesus who keeps them from the hell they are headed to, but not the Jesus who delivers them from the hell they are living in. Jesus is a healer; he wants to heal our inner woundedness. He wants to get to our inner being in the deepest part of who we are. It is the process of sanctification."

Beginning Celebrate Recovery

Because the leaders at Grace Church value healthy processes, they decided to launch their recovery ministry using Celebrate Recovery, an established, church-based recovery ministry tool created by John Baker at Saddleback Church in Lake Forest, California. In 1991, John Baker launched Celebrate Recovery (CR) with fewer than fifty people. It was created as a program to help those struggling with "hurts, habits, and hang-ups" engage in a recovery process that introduced them to God's mercy and grace and Jesus' healing power. Today churches all over the world use the materials of Celebrate Recovery to guide them in offering this recovery ministry model to their communities. The purpose of CR is to encourage fellowship and to celebrate God's healing power as participants work their way along the road to recovery. By working through the twelve steps and eight principles of Celebrate Recovery (see appendix C), people grow spiritually and find hope that they can experience freedom from their issues. This is achieved through praise, worship, informative lessons, personal testimonies, fellowship, and small groups.

Small groups are tailored to address the particular needs of people. At Grace Church, groups are available to help people with a variety of different needs: anger; chemical dependency; codependency; financial problems; food addictions; nicotine addiction; physical, emotional, and sexual abuse; sexual addiction; and love and relationship addictions. Grace Church's recovery ministry is an integral part of the church body. From the top down, people are willing to enter into the difficult process of acknowledging their own defects of character, and they will go to any lengths to experience restoration.

As Grace Church began hosting Celebrate Recovery groups at the church, they noticed some dramatic changes. "Every Friday night at two of our campuses and every Tuesday night at the other, we get a front-row seat to life change," says Jorge. Now, every two months when they hold baptism services, they are frequently baptizing several dozen new followers of Jesus. Six days a week, the church is helping people through the process of recovery through step studies, recovery Bible studies, and secular recovery groups.

The Messy Work of Restoring the Soul

Recovery is a process. It's not always easy. There are successes and failures, and it often takes time for people to really change. Jorge frequently asks, "How long did it take for the Devil to screw up your life? How long will you give Jesus to clean up your life?" Jorge finds encouragement in Jesus' example: "Remember that Jesus' twelve disciples walked with him for three years and they still didn't get it completely." Often at Grace, there are people who relapse into old habits and patterns of sin. They may stand up and walk out of the gathering in the middle of a sermon to take a smoke break, or bring their crying babies into the sanctuary during the message.[24] For a lot of traditional church people, Grace Church feels a bit too raw. Jorge agrees that it's a messy church, but he considers it a "divine, incarnational mess." Jesus' message needs to be incarnated into a messy world, a world that places little value on eternal spiritual truth. "I've switched my addiction from something that destroys life (alcohol) to a much better addiction, an addiction to seeing lives transformed by God's power."

Today if you walk into the sanctuary at Grace Church, you're likely to notice the coffee stains on the floor of the sanctuary. Jorge doesn't like to have them there, but he sees in them a picture of the message he is trying to share with the church. A sanctuary with coffee stains is a powerful reminder to us that God works in some of the messiest places. We don't need to get cleaned up to experience him; his love and his empowering grace are what transform us and bring healing.

Evangelistic Impact

Over the years, Grace Church has created a new environment, a place that provides the time, the people, and the right process for Jesus' healing ministry to be worked into lives. Evangelism flourishes at their recovery meetings. "The fish almost jump into the boat," says Jorge. Often people with no faith in Christ come to one of their healing ministries and surrender their lives to Jesus on the spot. They come to the meeting with a need for healing, and in the process they meet the Healer. Jorge believes that ministry to the "least of these" may be the great *omission* of the church today, but he is encouraged to see that some things are changing. "There is a stirring in churches of all theological stripes to wed a red-hot passion for personal evangelism and discipleship with a compassionate love for the poor, marginalized, and addicted. The world is standing on tippy-toe to see this kind of church!"[25]

The people of Grace Church have not only embraced the healing ministry of recovery in their midst but also begun caring for the community outside the church walls. Most of Grace's externally focused ministries are run by volunteers. Jorge explains, "Jesus did not come to reach the healthy; he came to the sick." Because of this, some church members have taken the initiative to start their own ministries. One woman in the church was called by God to care for and minister to exotic dancers and prostitutes. She is building a team to do just that. This is not a ministry that was assigned to her; it is a ministry that she was called to by God. "We are smaller than we could be because we have chosen this way of ministry of going after those no one sees or wants, but we think it is the way Jesus ministered," Jorge says. His simple prayer — "send us the people nobody else wants" — is being answered, and lives are being transformed by God's grace.

Creativity Encourages Growth

Every growing church pushes against certain constraints — the size of the facility, the church budget, the amount of land, the requirements of city ordinances, just to name a few. Vision and creativity are often needed to overcome these constraints. Grace Church serves as an example for other churches wanting to have a broader kingdom impact. They are reaching the people no one else is reaching and are expanding the ministry of the church beyond their church building.

In 2003, Grace Church adopted a shrinking and dying congregation in a nearby community and, in doing so, inadvertently launched their first multisite campus at Fort Myers Shores. When the Fort Myers Shores campus became a part of Grace Church, it adopted Grace's vision: "To partner with God in transforming people from unbelievers to fully devoted disciples of Jesus, to the glory of God." About twenty-five Cape Coral members decided to make a two-year commitment to join those at the Fort Myers Shores campus to launch this new effort. One of the first decisions they made was to remove the For Church Use Only sign on the basketball court. The church would be for the community, not just the church. Soon kids from the community began playing sports on the new campus, and today more than a hundred kids and teens are involved in a sports ministry. Eventually Grace added another campus, yet even as the church grew and expanded, they kept their focus on reaching out to the large numbers of addicted and broken people in their community.

In 2006, the Cape Coral campus of Grace Church realized that it wasn't enough for them to simply focus on getting people saved and sober. They decided to address other issues, such as unemployment, education, hunger, and even gang violence. This holy discontent stirred up the church, and in September of that same year, Grace Community Center (*www.egracecenter.org*) was born.

Grace Community Center is a place where people can hear the good news and find healing. After acquiring an abandoned Winn Dixie Superstore, they transformed the 56,000-square-foot facility into a meeting place that seats more than a thousand people and houses free and reduced-fee medical care, vocational training, a Meals on Wheels program, an after-school program for at-risk youth, a food bank, GED training, and a computer lab. Revenue for the center is provided by a thrift store, a coffee shop, a moving company, and a bookstore — all supported by and housed in the community center.

Grace Community Center also offers dance classes twice a week, parenting classes on Saturdays, and ministry to the homeless on Wednesdays and runs a thriving sports ministry throughout the week. Once a month, they help the unemployed and underemployed by giving away two to three tons of food, free haircuts, and a thousand articles of clothing. They regularly provide medical screenings and referrals and through all this are helping to restore the soul of their community.

Not Accidental or Haphazard

Although Grace Church has developed a unique connection between their recovery ministry and the use of multiple sites to facilitate growth, the distinctive lessons that Grace Church offers come not so much from their organizational structure as from the commitment that Jorge and his teams have made to filter all their decisions through their core values and their own experiences.

To an outsider, it might appear that Grace Church does much of their ministry spontaneously, even accidentally! But this can be misleading. The decisions they make are not haphazard or random. Every decision is made in light of the overall vision and is guided by an established process. Shaped by John Wesley's commitment to methods, they follow a simple strategy: "For each wave of grace, there was a corresponding formative element to connect people to that grace."[26] Grace Church's processes serve as the "corresponding formative element[s]" to make grace operational in the lives of people. To implement these methods of connecting people to God's grace, the church is committed to a four-stage process:

1. *Reach.* Ministries that engage and invite unchurched people in our community to experience the love of Jesus through the body of Christ. "Go to the street corners and invite to the banquet anyone you find" (Matt. 22:9).

2. *Connect.* Ministries that help people connect relationally and belong in the Grace Church family. "All the believers devoted themselves to the apostles' teaching, and to fellowship, and to sharing in meals (including the Lord's Supper), and to prayer.... They worshiped together at the Temple each day, met in homes for the Lord's Supper, and shared their meals with great joy and generosity — all the while praising God and enjoying the goodwill of all the people. And each day the Lord

added to their fellowship those who were being saved"
(Acts 2:42, 46 – 47 NLT).

3. *Form.* Ministries that help people have a growing and
transforming relationship with Jesus Christ. "O LORD,
you are our Father. We are the clay, and you are the pot-
ter. We all are formed by your hand" (Isa. 64:8 NLT).

4. *Send.* Ministries that release God's people to make the
realities of heaven the realities of earth. "Jesus said,
'Peace be with you! As the Father has sent me, I am
sending you'" (John 20:21).[27]

This four-stage process serves as a grid for all decisions related to
evangelism and discipleship and orients the church in a consistent
direction. But as beneficial as it is to have a clear process, it doesn't
eliminate the unpredictability that comes with change. Along with
an established process, the personal experience of the staff and leadership provides them with the wisdom and discernment they need to
effectively minister to people. While the process provides the broad
direction for making decisions, it is the people and their experience
that provide the wisdom needed to address the messy, unpredictable
nature of recovery ministry.

The Right People Make the Process Work

More than anything else, the decision to begin a recovery ministry
at Grace was a strategic one, an extension of the lives of its members
and leaders. Jorge's life is a great example of this. He regularly speaks
about his family of origin and how his dysfunctional family shaped
his beliefs and actions. His family background and personal experience make him an effective minister as he seeks to serve those people
others neither see nor want.

Having the right leadership — the right people in place — is an
essential part of having an effective recovery ministry. In December
of 2004, John Leonard became the leader of Celebrate Recovery at
Grace Church. What made John the right person for that job? Again,
it was his history, his personal experience of coming through the

recovery process. John's experience of recovery from sinful patterns and habits has uniquely equipped him to embrace those who come to Grace Church looking for help. He shares, "When I came into recovery, I thought I only had a drinking problem; what I really had was a thinking problem. Drinking and drugging were mere symptoms of my real problem — not having a relationship with God. The whole purpose of working the steps was to draw me closer to God, and to learn to rely on him to help me through my problems."

The experiences of Jorge and John have blessed them with eyes to see how God may be working in the lives of people others might miss or overlook. Their experience also has taught them to wait patiently, to trust that God does indeed transform people and equip them for ministry. Their own rocky roads to recovery provide them with the faith and humility that are needed to support this vision through repeated disappointment — and success. Recovery ministry leaders must come to understand that their calling is not primarily about managing behavior; it's about soul repair.

The People Everyone Wants

Heather was a stripper who began attending the Celebrate Recovery classes at Grace Church in 2005. When she was just nine years old, a traumatic experience changed the trajectory of her life. When she was in charge of babysitting her two brothers while her dad was away at work and her mom was studying in her room, Heather's four-year-old brother, Zachary, wandered into the back yard and drowned in the family's algae-infested, unkempt swimming pool. Though there was an investigation by the Department of Children and Families after the funeral and Heather and her parents were cleared of any charges, Heather was constantly haunted by her grief and guilt. Her family soon moved to the Cape Coral community and never again talked about what happened, but the pain remained, buried deep in her heart. Heather recalls trying to commit suicide as a young child by taking prescription acne medication, but she was unsuccessful. Her parents tried to cope with her behavior by keeping her busy with cheerleading, dance classes, and acting and singing lessons.

By the time she was in middle school, Heather was leading a

double life as captain of the cheerleading team and a juvenile delinquent. She skipped school, eventually dropping out in tenth grade and becoming a runaway and a drug dealer. Frequently abused and promiscuous, Heather ran into trouble with the law and was sent to rehab as part of her sentencing. Though she left rehab and never used drugs again, her troubles continued. She soon found work at a local strip club, a trailer with a pole and a jukebox. She became a featured dancer for the club.

Eventually Heather became pregnant. She dumped her drug-addicted boyfriend and did the best she could to raise her son but continued to strip as a means of supporting her family. Soon, though, her son became extremely ill, and he ended up in a coma for two long months. It was during this time that God met Heather in a small chapel near the hospital where her son was being treated. "I passed a chapel ten times a day every day, thinking to myself as I saw people crying and praying, 'What fools!' ... This time the chapel was empty, and I went in the chapel to tell God off. I was literally kicking and screaming for about twenty minutes. God and I got into a big fight that day. I just walked out and dismissed it. I took the hospital elevator up to my son's room, and everyone was in there. He was sitting up eating a popsicle! He was going to live! I didn't realize it until months later that God must have really listened to me."

In time, God provided Heather with a way out of her stripping career. One night, while working at the club, Heather found herself praying as she sat on the floor in front of a toilet. She desperately knew that she had to turn her life around, but she felt lost and alone. As she left that prayer session, preparing to take her place on the dance floor, she accidentally bumped into a man who took the time to listen to her story and provided her with the way out she had been looking for. Through some financial gifts, Heather was able to start down a new career path and has never danced again. In a strange twist of events, God delivered Heather from her situation by using a man who was there to enjoy the show.

Heather and countless others like her remind us that hurting people are not abandoned by God. Before she ever came to Grace Church, God had already reached out to Heather, teaching her that he was both willing and able to save her. When Heather began attending the Celebrate Recovery meetings at Grace Church, she discovered a place where she could share her story, and she began to find the healing she needed. It was at one of the Celebrate Recovery meetings that Heather was finally able to grieve the loss of her brother, eighteen years later. Today she is a loving mom and a successful businesswoman.

Grace Church has learned that by God's grace, the people nobody wants can become people everyone wants, people whose lives overflow with the love of God. Though it is often difficult to welcome the people no one else wants or sees, Grace Church is blessed to have a front-row seat to watch God at work. Every day, they are seeing God transform and heal hurting people through the ministries of the church.

Questions for Reflection and Discussion

1. Cape Coral was a city of contradictions: beautiful and charming yet financially distressed and crime-ridden. What contradictions exist in your city?

2. What contradictions exist in the community surrounding your church?

3. What contradictions exist within your congregation?

4. Who might be the right people to lead recovery ministries in your church?

5. What are the "qualifiers" for ministry?

6. Grace Church took down the playground sign that read For Church Use Only. It was a simple change marking a huge paradigm shift. Are there any "signs" that need to change at your church? What simple changes might you make to reflect a value of restoring a community and souls, not just a church?

chapter eight

A FAMILY OF TRUST

Golden Gate Missionary Baptist Church

> We want to be a place where real life change takes place. When we see these lives change, when we see people get free, it keeps us from becoming complacent. It does something to the church as a whole; it gives us life.
>
> — *Pastor Vincent Parker*

CALVIN HAD TRIED HARD TO DO THE RIGHT THING. He had been blessed with a family who loved him and a recovery group that was helping him through his struggle with alcohol, yet despite his many valiant attempts at sobriety, Calvin had spent most of his life in and out of jail. He was a desperate man.

And sadly, Calvin was not one of the fortunate ones — those who make it through the hard times, stay in the recovery program, and eventually find release from the addictions that have taken them captive. In his late fifties, having struggled most of his life fighting his addictions, Calvin died in his jail cell from complications related to liver disease. When Calvin's family was informed of his death, they called Golden Gate Missionary Baptist Church and asked the pastors there if they would perform his service.

While none of Calvin's family members attended Golden Gate, they knew that the church had been an important part of Calvin's life. In their words, the only times that Calvin had been "clean and free and really happy" were when he was attending the church. Calvin had been a part of the recovery ministry at Golden Gate, but he had been more than that. Golden Gate had been his family.

Golden Gate Missionary Baptist Church is an African American church in Dallas, Texas. When most people think of Dallas, they think of affluence — the downtown skyline, The Galleria, and Highland Park. The Dallas metroplex has more stores and shopping centers per capita than any other US city or metropolitan area.[28] Yet while it is true that there are affluent areas in Dallas where some of the wealthiest families in the nation reside, there are also parts of the city on the lower end of the socioeconomic scale. Golden Gate was founded eighty years ago in a Dallas neighborhood known as The Bottom, a title it received because it was located behind a levy in the lowest part of the city. When the church was founded in 1930, in an era when racism and segregation were common in the South, The Bottom was one of the neighborhoods where African Americans could reside and thrive. Golden Gate started in The Bottom and has stayed there ever since.

Golden Gate has a membership of three thousand people and a regular weekend worship attendance of more than five hundred. The church has a wonderful history of faith in God and love for people, a faith and love that have been expressed down through the years through the outreach program that began decades ago. From the beginning, Golden Gate decided that their church was not just a *place* in the community; their church *was* the community.

The Rev. Dr. C. B. T. Smith was the pastor of Golden Gate for forty-five years, from 1952 to 1997. From the inception of his ministry, the congregation understood certain core beliefs about the place of the church. As Rable Johnson, head of the church deacons, explained, "The church is the community. You've got everything from lawyers and doctors to scrubs and nubs. He [Reverend Smith] felt like we should be able to reach and teach what we call the lowest of the low and the highest of the high."[29] So under the compassionate leadership of Reverend Smith, Golden Gate began to do just that — reaching out and teaching God's Word across socioeconomic and cultural barriers.

Reality Informs Opportunity

The church started an outreach ministry to the surrounding community because they saw firsthand the desperate needs of people. The community had a large number of homeless men, and during the 1980s, when drugs became readily available, the church realized that the most daunting roadblock to ministering to these homeless men was their growing dependence on alcohol and drugs. Unless the church could answer this problem, they weren't going to be able to make much progress. At the time, Reverend Smith felt called by God to do something. He believed that the church needed to find a way to assist addicts who wanted to break free from addictions to alcohol and drugs. From the earliest days, as the church ministered to the homeless men in The Bottom, their outreach to the community took on the character of recovery ministry, helping people experience freedom and healing from addictions.

Golden Gate started by hosting a twelve-step recovery meeting at the church. One of their deacons, an alcoholic who was fifteen years sober, would gather the men at the church and after the meeting shuttle them back to the various shelters they called home. It didn't take long for the church to realize that this approach was having minimal impact on the men. Though the men would show up at the meeting, they quickly reverted to their addictive behaviors, so the church leadership decided to provide more structure for the men and give them additional accountability. Within six months, they had rented a home to house a few of the addicted men attending the meetings. This was the initial step in launching an in-house program for addicts in recovery, called Adult Rehabilitation Ministry (ARM), a ministry that grew as the church moved from renting homes to buying homes. While the men lived in the homes, the leaders provided more consistent encouragement, love, discipleship, and recovery, and with the initiation of this new ministry, they started to see long-term change. Men began taking responsibility for their jobs, their marriages, and their families.

From the very start of the program, the men living in the ARM homes were considered a part of the church, members of God's family. The men were involved in whatever the church was doing, working with church members to serve one another and reach out to the community. Pastor Vincent Parker, the current pastor at Golden Gate, explains, "There is a sense that we are a family in our church — from the leadership in the pulpit on down. This [the ARM ministry] is not just a ministry on the side." If you walked into the church today, you would be hard-pressed to distinguish the men involved in the ARM program from the other church members. This inclusion of the men is an extension of God's grace, freely given to each of us. "From the moment you walk in," Pastor Parker says, "you are trusted. You don't have to earn it. You are given dignity because people believe in you. They are like your mom, your dad, your big brother, or your grandmother. They'll fuss at you if you mess up, but they love on you too."

Hope in Transformation

Pastor Parker, who came to serve at Golden Gate following Reverend Smith, knows that one of the reasons why his church has developed this culture of acceptance and love for addicts and homeless men is because virtually everyone in the church has someone — a family member, close friend, or relative — who struggles with substance abuse. Watching God change lives through the work of ARM gives them encouragement and hope that their loved ones might still have a chance at finding a new life.

Still, not every story ends in success.

When Pastor Parker was asked to do the funeral service for Calvin, he did so gladly, knowing that Calvin was strong in the Word of God and that he had made many attempts to follow after God. Because Pastor Parker understood the nature of addiction and had witnessed firsthand the commitment of men like Calvin, he was able to bring dignity and hope to the funeral of this man. For Pastor Parker and the members of Golden Gate, Calvin's funeral was a wonderful testimony, an encouragement to them that people feel so loved at Golden Gate that even when they haven't gotten their lives together, others still see that the church is a place where people are cared for and are able to experience God's love and grace, even as they struggle. Pastor Parker believes that his experience working with these men has also made him a better pastor. "Everybody has something going on in their lives that they are not dealing with. There are some closets that God has not been allowed into, and I have discovered that if you do not open up those closets to the Spirit of God through the Word of God, they will eat you up ... and sooner or later or you will spend your life pretending."

Pastor Vincent Parker began his ministry at Golden Gate with a deep passion to minister to and disciple African American men, to see them come to Christ, grow in their relationship with God, restore their families, and become leaders in their homes. "My interest was not so much in the area of drug rehabilitation, but I knew that 75 percent of African American kids grow up without men in the home. This scarcity of men in African American families is what motivated me to want to get involved." Parker became the director of the ministry of recovery after two years of working at the church. He turned to the volunteer leaders, those who had been working through their own journeys of recovery from addiction and were now leading others, and asked them to help him understand this community of men and learn how he could best minister to them.

He discovered that he was more like the people he came to serve than he had realized. "First of all, I had to learn that I was just like them," explains Parker. "When you scratch beneath the surface of the addiction, I am just like they are. The abuse of drugs was simply an external factor. These men had the same hurts, struggles, and dreams, but they made some decisions along the way that led them to use drugs. As a man, a human being living in a sin-filled world, I have the same struggles, passions, and temptations, and I still need to bring my passions under the control of the Holy Spirit today, just like they do. We are all the same at the basic level." Pastor Parker realized that if the men felt that he was speaking down to them or conveying that he was somehow better than them, his words would lack credibility and authenticity. Because many of these men have spent a lifetime hiding who they really are, they understand the scam. "A leader has got to be honest with his own stuff. We have our own struggles as pastors. You've got to be real. They need to know you are in the struggle too."

From Healing to Healer

Obie Bussey is a living testimony of the ministry of Golden Gate. While Reverend Smith laid a foundation for the ministry of recovery by emphasizing that the church is the community, and Pastor Parker has built on that by creating a family bond between ARM and the church, Obie is the blessed recipient of all of it. He has personally benefited from the nurture, love, hope, and dignity that this family has given to its children.

Obie was twelve years old when he started using drugs. "I vividly remember my summer after sixth grade. That summer I used to smoke weed and drink every day, right up until I came into the program. That was just what we did, all through middle school, all through high school. We used." The fraternal twins of drugs and alcohol escorted Obie into a life he never wanted. "I used crack cocaine and quickly became addicted and homeless, went to jail ... went to prison, and in 1989 I went to a homeless shelter called the Adult Life Foundation, where Golden Gate Baptist Church was doing street ministry and feeding the homeless." It was that day that Obie recognized a classmate from high school. His friend was leading the street ministry, and as they got reacquainted, his friend invited him to join the fellowship of Golden Gate. That moment was the beginning of Obie's transformation. Over the next nine years, Obie worked through his addictions and began reaching out to others who also were struggling with drugs and alcohol. Then, in 1996, he became an assistant director for the ministry, and by 1998 he was serving as the executive director. "When I came into the program at twenty-eight, I had never had a formal job that I had worked at for any length of time. So when I came into the program in 1989, it was the beginning of a complete transformation for me."

Home for the Homeless

Over the years, Golden Gate has become a home to those without a home, a family where people form relationships of trust, love, and accountability with one another. And like any family, the people at Golden Gate strive to stay healthy. Healthy families, at their best, create an environment that fosters the development of its members so they can live the life God intended. Parents teach their children how to love God with all their heart, soul, and strength (see Deut. 6:5). They teach them life skills. They guide them in resolving the problems that inevitably arise when humans live together. They help children appropriately express, understand, and resolve their emotions. Parents become students of their children and provide them with affirmation and support as they grow and mature, guiding them toward the life God wants for them. And in the healthiest of families is a deep well of grace.

Having been raised in the Golden Gate family, Obie knows what a healthy church family must do to help people move from a place of brokenness to healing and restoration. He emphasizes four key elements that characterize a healthy church family, one that welcomes those in need and empowers them to find hope to overcome their addictions.

1. Healthy families respect each other, trust each other, and treat each other with dignity. Obie has fond memories of his early days at Golden Gate. He recalls, "I was not treated as a 'client' or a program member. The folks at Golden Gate treated me like family. They treated me like I had some value and significance. They treated me like a person who was important. I wasn't a second-class anything. I was treated with dignity and respect."

At Golden Gate, if someone stumbles, the church family responds by helping that person regain their footing. Stumbling and setbacks are not causes for shaming or judgment but simply serve as a feedback mechanism, revealing where a person needs growth, help, and encouragement. According to Obie's estimation, more than 35 percent of the congregation have come through the recovery ministry, so there is a widespread understanding of the challenge of breaking free from addictions. Obie describes what it's like to come into the church through the recovery program: "At our church, you don't carry the stigma of, 'You're a former addict, so you can't do this or that....' When you complete [the program], and if you are faithful to stay clean and sober, you're allowed to grow in the church without the stigma of the program."

This ready acceptance of people, regardless of their past, is a vital part of Golden Gate's DNA. "In our church, a person is given full trust the day you walk in. You don't have to earn it. As we say, when you join in the recovery process, you have every right and responsibility in the church, so we have people singing in the choir, they go to Sunday School ... they're doing everything that anybody else does."

A healthy family also includes a large contingent of relatives who keep an eye out for everyone else. "The women of the church ... the mothers of the church, treat you like you're one of their kids, and that feels real good. They'll scold you when you mess up, but at the same time they'll love you and bake you cakes," says Obie, laughing. He is quick to admit that this type of grace and trust is not what people deserve. "A lot of men like me haven't felt that type of trust and love for a long time ... not even at home. Sometimes rightfully so, because we stole and we've done things that have torn that trust down. So it's not like people haven't got a reason for not trusting, but here ... well, here ... they trust you."

2. Healthy families love big but start small. Like most effective churches, Golden Gate follows the breadcrumbs and goes where God seems to be leading them. Since they walk by faith and not by sight, the path ahead often becomes clear only after they have walked it. Obie says, "I ask our deacons and elders all the time that if they had known how much the program would cost in the beginning, would they ever have done it?" In hindsight, they admit that they never would have started a ministry program knowing that it would eventually take up 40 percent of the church's budget! But they didn't start there. Instead, they started small, following the Holy Spirit's prompting and simply going out and feeding people, loving them, and teaching them God's Word.

Following the success of the ARM program, a partnership was formed with the Restoration Outreach of Dallas (ROD). Started by LeBalanc and Butch McCashlin, ROD is a comprehensive program that begins nine months before a prisoner is released and continues after they are out of prison. To be admitted into the program, each prisoner must want to experience positive change and is then required to attend three months of discipleship classes and participate in substance abuse programs if necessary. By offering ongoing, residential care for prisoners after they are released from prison,

ROD helps ex-offenders become chemical-free through a Christ-centered twelve-step program. ROD helps them with practical skills like resume writing, job referrals, and assistance in obtaining driver's licenses or Social Security cards. Residents have access to regular medical care and weekly support groups for themselves and their families. Because the leaders of ROD believe that permanent change is closely tied to following Jesus, discipleship is a critical component of all phases of the program.

Of the six hundred thousand individuals released from prison every year, 67 percent will be reincarcerated within three years. Amazingly, more than 80 percent of inmates have committed a drug-related crime. So without some type of life change, the chances for successful reentry into society are not good. And although many churches and individuals are working with inmates in our nation's jails and prisons, organized aftercare is still quite rare in most communities.

That's the difference a program like ROD makes in the lives of these men.

Living on-site for up to a year allows adults to work and save enough money so that upon completion of the program, they can afford to get their own apartment. Through the love expressed by staff and faithful volunteers, the hope of the gospel comes alive, and at-risk men and women become self-sufficient and fully contributing members of the community.

Obie was one of the first residents to participate in the program, which has since grown into a multiunit residential facility. "They started small. They loved big, but they started small. And through their faithfulness, the program grew. When my church sees me and my wife and my children growing in ministry, they have seen true life change and they have assisted. There is no joy to a believer greater than that."

3. Healthy families believe that prodigals still return home. Obie knows that recovery ministry is difficult work. It requires a deep commitment from both the church family and the individual in need of recovery. He explains, "When a person starts using, that's when they stop maturing. So whatever age they are when they start using, that's the age they are emotionally stuck at." Obie remembers his own struggle when he first started in the program. "So here I was, coming into the program, a twenty-eight-year-old man ... but from an emotional standpoint, I operated and responded to life like a twelve-year-old because I didn't have the basic living skills. So you're looking at me as a fully grown man, but emotionally I'm like a teenager." This understanding helps to explain why the relapse rate in the program is still so high, even for a successful program like the one at Golden Gate. The national average for relapse in recovery programs is about 98 percent; only about 2 percent end up staying clean the first time through a program. But at Golden Gate the relapse rate is around 40 percent. Still, Obie is slow to celebrate that statistic. "Even at 60 percent success, you still have 40 percent relapsing."

What happens to those who relapse again and again? "For me, when I came in 1989, I relapsed real quickly five times. I was not one of the people who got it the first time. But my church and my mentors stuck with me through five times of relapse." According to Obie, that's what healthy families do. The faithful perseverance and patience of church members who hung in with him through multiple relapses was a great encouragement to him and serves as a model for his own ministry today. Even during his fourth and fifth relapses, his church family believed that God was both able and willing to save him, that every life is worthy of redemption. Obie reminds us that families — healthy, strong families — fight for the well-being of their kids. It's not always easy to keep the faith. But thankfully, God not only delivers the addicted in his timing; he also encourages those who stand with them in battle. Obie is inspired by the promise of Philippians 2:13: "It is God who works in you to will and to act according to his good purpose." And he doesn't have to look very far to be reminded that God is faithful, even when it seems impossible. "Our church is made up of former clients and their families. I think we have maybe ten associate ministers on our roster, and probably six of them are former clients. We have two deacons who have come through the recovery program."

With patience comes lasting fruit.

4. *Healthy families know it takes a village.* The leaders at Golden Gate know that nobody makes it on their own. We all need supportive "siblings" who will help us out along the way. "When a man

comes into the program, we ask him to get a support group — those who stand with you in your recovery. These relationships should be lifelong. The same support group that I had in 1989, I still have today. These are my partners, friends, and mentors," says Obie. Ideally, support groups consist of four or five others. As the adage says, "It takes a village to raise a child," and the leaders at Golden Gate have adopted a similar approach to raising up and discipling children of faith.

Relationships at Golden Gate aren't short-term commitments. People are committed to the long haul, to seeing it through to the end. Because of the longevity of the relationships at the church, those who commit themselves to the ministry of recovery often see some wonderful results. Obie explains, "Only yesterday, a group of guys who came through the program under me went out to dinner, something we do every other month. To go to a restaurant and watch guys who came into the program homes, addicted to drugs, unemployed and probably unemployable ... to see these same guys, now employed, drive up in their cars, to get out and to just be able to do normal things ... it never gets old. To see them own their own homes, marry, have families, and work in ministry themselves — those are the blessings of my calling. I don't think anything is more beautiful than watching someone who could not live and function, to be able to change; to watch that transformation take place. You get to see people transformed."

Obie and his church believe in transformation because they have seen it happen. Each day, they are surrounded by the evidence of God's faithfulness and are reminded that the work they do is not in vain. As the director of recovery, Obie understands in a personal way the satisfaction described by the apostle John: "I have no greater joy than to hear that my children are walking in the truth" (3 John 1:4). Seeds sown years ago are now bearing fruit for God's kingdom.

Questions for Reflection and Discussion

1. Who have you seen overcome an issue and transform into a passionate leader like Obie?

2. In what ways does your church model a family?

3. Trust is a big deal at Golden Gate, and they give it from the start. What about your church? On a scale of one to ten, how trusting of new people is your church? (One being trust is almost nonexistent with new people, ten being new and seasoned members are trusted the same.)

4. Which impression do you most often give to others: "I've got it all together" or "I'm a work in progress too"?

chapter nine

A CHURCH WITHIN A CHURCH

Mercy Street Church

> Grace is just a five-letter word until I tell you my experience about being lost in darkness, painfully alone in my addiction, and how God found me through an encounter with another addict at a coffee shop. It was on that day that grace moved beyond theology for me and became autobiography.
>
> — *Pastor Matt Russell*

WHEN THE SENIOR PASTOR of Chapelwood United Methodist Church asked his newest staff member, Matt Russell, what he would like to do at the church, Matt's reply was anything but typical. "I want to figure out how to connect with people who see church as irrelevant in their lives," Matt said. "Can you give me the phone number of the guy who was the *most* pissed when he left the church?"

The result of that phone call was Mercy Street.

Mercy Street was introduced to me (Liz) as "a church within a church." It's a weekly service that meets at Chapelwood United Methodist Church in Houston, Texas, every Saturday night. The neighborhood around Chapelwood is marked by well-manicured lawns, stately architecture, and expensive cars. But at Mercy Street Church, you'll find many of those same automobiles parked alongside a colorful array of old buses, rusting pickup trucks, and a few scattered Harleys. You'll likely find a group gathering to smoke by the entrance, along with a few individuals decked out in tattoos and leather standing in the lobby. You'll also find a good number of "normies" interspersed. In recovery language, a normie is an individual who might not fit the expected recovery profile (in other words, he looks normal, whatever that may mean). People who attend Mercy Street run the entire spectrum — from lawyers and bankers to homeless men and women living on the street. To understand why all these people are gathering at a place like Chapelwood, you need to start by learning the story of the man who founded Mercy Street, Matt Russell.

The Jesus Movement

Matt's parents were the product of a movement in the 1970s known as the Jesus Movement, and as a result, he entered the life of church through a different door than did your typical Christian. Matt's first introduction to church was a halfway house in Dallas. Every Sunday, he joined his parents as they met at their church, a place filled with interesting people, people he really enjoyed. At the time, he had no idea that his parents were communing with individuals who were struggling with addictions and deep brokenness. He just knew that he liked hanging around them. After leaving the halfway house, the family attended and eventually joined a more traditional church, leaving Matt somewhat confused. He wondered what had happened to the other people, the ones who were so easy to talk with.

At their new church, Matt was taught to understand what the church should be and what he ought to do to be a good Christian. But for some reason, it all seemed so unnatural to him. Still, as time went by, he assimilated into the life of this new congregation. Then, Matt and his father experienced a devastating loss; Matt's mother learned she had brain cancer, and she grew extremely sick. Desperately trying to make sense of what was happening to his mother, Matt began asking people, "Why would God allow this to happen?" Responding to Matt's cries for understanding, various church members told him that "there must be sin in your mother's life" or "she is most likely an unsubmissive wife." At the time, Matt knew that the answers were not only wrong; they were cruel and insensitive. In frustration, he ended up leaving the church, angry at God, angry at God's people, and deeply wounded. What Matt had needed was hope and comfort; instead, he was abandoned to walk alone through his grief and loss after his mother died. Matt tried to figure out how to make sense of all that was going on in his life. But the pain remained, and the only way he could cope was by dulling it with drugs. Though Matt began using, he didn't consider himself an addict. After all, he had been raised in a good neighborhood, he didn't live under a bridge, and he continued to go to school and pursue ambitious goals. Matt soon entered college and excelled in his classes. He seemed to be doing fine, as long as he could occasionally "numb out" when necessary to dull his inner pain.

A Transforming Relationship

One day, while sitting in a school committee meeting, Matt struck up a relationship with another committee member named Jim. When the meeting ended, Jim invited Matt to visit him at his office. He gave Matt directions and they set a time to meet, but when Matt arrived, he realized that Jim didn't work in the business world; he was employed at a church. Not only that, but he was actually the senior pastor for a megachurch numbering several thousand people. Wondering if he had been set up, Matt cautiously entered Jim's office. Much to Matt's surprise, Jim did not try to talk him into coming back to church or hammer him on the head with religious teaching. Instead, Jim asked a few questions and gave Matt a chance to talk. "He let me come in every week for about an hour and a half," Matt said, "and I just puked up my life on his tennis shoes." For the next two months, they met and Matt talked about his experience with the church and his former faith and let out all of his complaints and criticisms. Jim sat attentively and just listened.

Matt was moved by the way Jim embraced and accepted him. "Here Jim was the pastor of a church with thousands of attendees, and he had lots to do, but he made time for me," he says. Matt had never anticipated this. He was even more stunned when, in the midst of all his confessions and complaints, Jim looked directly into Matt's eyes and said, "I think you need to be a pastor." Matt thought that Jim needed to stop smoking crack, and he told him so. How in the world could this guy, who had just spent several weeks listening to Matt attack the church, say such a ridiculous thing? He had been very direct with Jim in expressing his disappointment in the church: "Church was a place where once you adopted the lingo of religion, you could hide from what was really happening. It wasn't a place where you could ask real questions like, 'What do you do with the problem of pain?' or 'What do you do when a baby dies?' or 'What do you do when a mother who is a wonderful person gets brain cancer?'" Matt complained to Jim that the church was not a place where people really struggle or deal with deep pains and failures. "I found that the church was not a safe place where you could deal with the darkness in your life. Once you were synchronized with the language of the church, you had access to the leadership positions. There was something about that that seemed very distorted to me."

Still, despite all Matt's criticisms of the church, Jim's words struck a chord within him.

Between Two Worlds

Matt finished his undergrad degree and decided to stay around for a year and get involved in a campus ministry "to test the waters." After he returned from a spring mission trip in Mexico with the campus ministry, the Mexican pastor they had served with called the church and asked Matt to consider an internship with him. Matt accepted the call and moved to Mexico, living with the Sisters of Mercy, the Catholic order founded by Mother Teresa. This was a group of women who were pulling kids out of the trash dumps and bringing them into the orphanage to receive care, love, and education. Matt also taught a group of young adults who were educated and financially secure. He began to realize that the integration of these two worlds was an important part of God's calling on his life, the challenge of bringing the lives of the privileged and the poor together. The experience of ministry in Mexico and the sense that these two very different socioeconomic worlds needed to come together ignited a passion in Matt's heart and solidified his desire to answer the call to full-time ministry.

After six months working in Mexico, Matt returned to California and enrolled at Fuller Theological Seminary, where one of his professors asked a question: "How far did Jesus actually descend into humanity to redeem us?" Matt found himself intrigued by the question. He contemplated the implications and sought God and the Scriptures for answers. After several weeks of study and self-examination, Matt concluded that he wanted to know more of Jesus, the one who, as Matt says, "descended into literal hell and also into the utter hell of our humanity, the one who reconciled us through that act and then redeemed us. The one who calls people to follow him came not with a message of shame but bringing us a message of liberty." Matt developed a theological sense of his calling and ministry based on this notion of Jesus and his descent into the depths of our humanity. What would it mean, Matt pondered, to be a pastor who would help people not only understand the theology of ascent and victory over sin and death but also grasp the theology of descent?

A theology of ascent often encourages faith in God's power and ability to help us through the hard times in life. It's a theology that encourages us when we struggle, by reminding us that we will, one day, get through these struggles and life will get better. It describes a life that moves up and to the right, a gradual progression lived in the hope that things will improve.

But a theology of ascent is incomplete. It must be balanced by a theology of descent, which recognizes that life, even a life committed to Christ, does not always move up and to the right. "I had always believed in the theology of ascent," Matt explained. "That's the normal evangelical testimony. However, there is a descent that is just as important as the ascent." The theology of descent is not, primarily, about our lives as human beings. It's about the movement of Jesus Christ, who descended from the glory of heaven and experienced death and the utter depths of our humanity. Because Jesus has descended to the depths of our human experience, he can now meet us at our darkest times. "A theology that recognizes the reality of death reflects human experience more accurately. Jesus knows the reality of our human depravity, and he brings his grace right into the middle of that reality, not just at salvation but as a process of sanctification, even as we are still being drawn into sin, faithlessness, and doubt."

Matt's growing convictions came from realizing that many Christians' experience did not reflect the traditional story of success and victory. Matt knew that many of these people deeply desired to experience Jesus as their redeemer and deliverer, yet their lives were far from exemplary. He knew that there were individuals who had walked away from the Christian faith because they never felt they could quite live up to the image of the perfect Christian living in the victory of the resurrection.

Matt wasn't simply wrestling with ideas. He was living them out in his personal life. During his studies at Fuller, preparing for ministry, he was living a dual life: seeking God, growing in his faith, and yet still depending on drugs to help him deal with his despair and loss. He had learned to keep a careful balance between his two seemingly contradictory lives, believing that as long as he trusted Christ to heal him, did his best, and hoped hard enough, things eventually would get better.

After Matt graduated from Fuller, Jim Jackson, the man who had challenged Matt to become a pastor in the first place, asked him to move to Houston and start working with him at his church, Chapelwood. Matt was given several responsibilities at first, but not long after he arrived, Jim asked him, "Matt, what do you want to do?"

Matt replied, "I want to figure out how to connect with people who see church as irrelevant in their lives."

Jim's answer was clear and to the point: "Go do it." So Matt decided to interview people who had left the church, with the hope of gaining insight into their lives. He set up office at a coffee shop in town and asked Jim if he could have the phone number of the guy who was most irritated (*pissed* was the exact word he used) when he left the church.

Jim gave Matt the phone number of a man named John. Though Matt made several calls to John and left his name and number, he heard nothing back. Finally he left a message promising that he wouldn't try to get John to come back to church, that he didn't want anything from John, but that he just wanted to hear John's story and ask a couple of questions. Matt promised to buy him a cup of coffee too. When John heard that message, he called Matt back and arranged to meet him for his free cup of coffee.

Matt listened as John began to describe his experience. John was an alcoholic. He had come to church because he was searching for hope and help and thought that the church was "a real hope-filled place." But John began to recognize that even though the church offered genuine hope in God, it was not a place where he could speak freely about the darkness he struggled with, particularly his struggle with alcoholism. When he would talk about his personal issues, he noticed that people listening would suddenly grow uncomfortable. He would sense that there was an invisible threshold he'd crossed in talking about his addiction to alcohol. John learned that it was okay to generalize about his sin and admit that we are all sinners and have issues, but he also learned that you couldn't be honest, real, and specific about your problems.

John happened to also be attending an Alcoholics Anonymous meeting at the time, and he couldn't understand why the people at that meeting, most of whom did not know the God of the Bible, welcomed him and accepted him just as he was, but the people at his church couldn't. At AA, he found a community that valued honesty, openness, and authenticity. He knew that at an AA meeting he could say what was really going on in his life, and people there would listen. And he found that he really needed a community that would help him heal and grow, and that needed to be a place where he was both known and accepted. Unfortunately for John, church was not that place.

As Matt listened to John's words, he began to realize that he himself needed the very same healing that John was experiencing in recovery through AA. In a strange and ironic twist of God's mercy, it was Matt's time with John — the angriest person ever to leave Chapelwood — that began the process of redemption in Matt's life, prompting his journey of recovery from addiction.

"Grace is just a five-letter word," Matt says, "until I tell you my experience about being lost in darkness, painfully alone in my addiction, and how God found me through an encounter with another addict at a coffee shop. It was on that day that grace moved beyond theology for me and became autobiography. And that movement of knowing *about* grace to encountering and being undone by grace has meant everything to me. For years I had talked about the concept of grace, written about it — even preached about it — but when it showed up across the table from me in the form of John S., I was forever changed by it."[30]

Matt continued interviewing people for more than a year. Altogether, he bought coffee for and listened to nearly sixty people. After concluding his interviews, he invited everyone he had talked with to a dinner he was hosting at a friend's house. Forty people showed up that night for dinner, and after the meal, Matt shared what he had learned through his interviews. He divided the topics into themes, wrote them on a flip chart, and facilitated a discussion. Matt had found that most of the reasons why people had left church or were refusing to go to church fit under six headings:

1. The church does not feel like a place where a person can be honest about his real struggles, issues, and sins.
2. Certain sins are acceptable to talk about in church, while other sins are not.
3. The church uses shame to motivate people to change.
4. People in church come across as fake and inauthentic.
5. To be accepted at church, a person has to invest a lot of time and effort in image management or giving the impression that one is doing great and living right, even when it is not true.
6. The church always asks for money.

After the discussion, Matt said to the group, "I want to share a model of church with you that might address your concerns. It would not be a place where a guy just told you how to live, but it would be a place where you could tell the truth about yourself and hear the truth about others without a sense of shame attached to it. It would be a place where you could process your life and where people could handle the mess you are in." He asked the group to take a week to think about it and see who would like to be a part of the group that would help create this kind of church.

A week later thirty-five of the original forty people came back for a second dinner, ready to invest their lives and time into this new endeavor. The group continued meeting every week after that for the next six months. Some of the members of the group were not even believers, yet they yearned for a place where they could seek God.

Six months later this small group of people launched Mercy Street, a church within a church, and started meeting on Saturday nights at Chapelwood. Before their first service, Jim Jackson invited Matt to come and stand with him in front of the Sunday service at Chapelwood, where Matt talked about his vision, his experience, and his hopes for the new church. He then asked if anyone in the large congregation would be willing to help out with and support this new church. Jim joined Matt in soliciting the support of the congregation, and there was a rousing response to the appeal for support. Seven hundred people showed up for the first service of Mercy Street Church: five hundred supporters from the larger church body and two hundred people from the surrounding community!

Mercy Street has now been a church for more than a decade, and Matt Russell has left Mercy Street to pursue further education. Even though Matt is gone, his role has been capably filled by Pastor Gregg Taylor. As the leaders at Mercy Street reflect on their past and continue planning for the future, the ministry team has learned some valuable lessons, principles for uniting the ministry of recovery and the work of the local church that can benefit any church with a heart to reach its community for Christ.

1. Recovery ministries challenge our notions on belief, belonging, community, and membership. The story of Mercy Street reminds us of the constant discrepancy we find between the typical testimony and the reality of most people's lives. Matt explains, "Most testimonies are stories about what happened in a person's life in the past, how God changed their lives in a dramatic way, and how they are so much better today than they were before. The problem is that such stories set a standard that many people cannot relate to or ever attain to. They cannot fit their present reality into a story that speaks of hardship as something that happened only in the past. It is true that people do come to Jesus and they have a life change, and that's cool, but that is not the only story about how Jesus works in a person's life."

Mercy Street is a collection of people who deeply desire to know God, but their stories don't necessarily fit into a "before, now, and after" narrative. That said, it's wrong to say that transformation is not occurring in their lives. Recovery, though, is less about the destination (in this life) and all about recognizing and embracing the journey. The goal of our perfection will not be complete until we see Jesus, but we must continue to live in God's acceptance, celebrating each day of the journey, even the days of failure and struggle.

Recovery ministries try to create an atmosphere in which shame is not welcome. This leads them to rejoice when people show up, even if they come in late and loud. A large smoking session outside a meeting is a cause for delight, not an excuse for a sermon on the evils of nicotine.

2. The church can help people struggle with profound issues of humanity and faith. Mercy Street has become a safe place for "spiritual refugees" in Houston's recovery community. Catholics, Southern Baptists, Eastern Orthodox, Presbyterians, and Pentecostals all hang out together at Mercy Street, along with Buddhists, agnostics, and a large number of people who feel uncomfortable checking off a particular denominational block on a census form. These are folks who consider themselves spiritual but not religious.

This open embrace of diverse spiritualities has typically made religious people pretty uneasy, even in the first century. When Jesus "became flesh and blood, and moved into the neighborhood" (John 1:14 MSG), many religious leaders were uncomfortable with his methodology. They had traditions and rules and expectations. Tensions arose as Jesus did new things and got unexpected results. He taught with an authority that amazed the crowds and caused many to believe. He drove out recalcitrant demons, and the mere grasp of his cloak could heal a debilitating disease. He fulfilled prophecies, raised the dead, and fed thousands out of a child's lunch satchel. But the most learned religious scholars of his day suggested he was in cahoots with the Enemy and plotted his death.

Jesus ministered in ways that the religious leaders of his day found offensive. They could not reconcile his story with their expectations of what should happen when the Messiah showed up. They followed the Law, sorting people into categories (clean vs. unclean, Gentile vs. Jew). This separation helped define the Jewish culture and maintain identity in a difficult cultural and political climate. Jesus, however, showed up and preached a kingdom of messiness. "Jesus ... was a revolutionary in that he advocated an outgoing holiness of healing and bridge-building rather than a defensive holiness of withdrawal."[31]

3. Recovery ministries blur denominational lines. Members of Mercy Street may even be members at other churches, often attending Mercy Street on Saturday evening and their home church on Sunday. Some who attend are church dropouts. Many are not liturgically housebroken or religiously savvy. In fact, faith-based recovery ministries like Mercy Street often find themselves adjusting to their unique membership — people who regularly break all the rules because they don't know them or don't care to follow them.

The greeting teams at most traditional churches hand you a bulletin, shake your hand, and offer to show you where to drop off your children on the way to worship. Walking into a recovery ministry is more like running the gauntlet. Those interested in getting inside often must weave their way through the smokers, an informal but still quite friendly greeting team. Children overload their paper plates with snacks and then leave behind a trail of cookies and salsa as they run for a seat. Preschoolers hang on to their mothers' jean-clad legs and refuse to be shuttled off to child care. No one gets all that concerned about the obvious chaos. Recovery ministry leaders eagerly open their doors wide to anyone willing to enter, regardless of how inconvenient the experience.

A good example of this attitude is Jerry, a man who first came to Mercy Street with his AA home group. He participated in the Recovery and Spirituality support group that followed the service, and volunteered for the van ministry team. Consistent, eager to serve, and generous, he was a congregant that any pastor would love. Jerry was a one-man outreach committee, bringing a slew of friends with him each week.

One night after the service, Jerry approached Matt with a broad smile and said, "Matt, I'd like to join Mercy Street."

"But Jerry, you're a Jew!" Matt said. He tried to reason with Jerry.

"I explained to him the best I could the theology of the church — that the church is an extension of Jesus' ongoing ministry of reconciliation to the world, that those who join the church are joining themselves to this person who was God and who proclaimed to be the Messiah and Savior not only of the Jews but also of the entire world. That membership in the church is a move toward solidarity with Jesus in the world. And although my mouth did not say it again, all I could think over and over again was, 'But Jerry, you're a Jew.'"

Although Jerry's request for membership startled Matt (a rookie minister), Jerry was clear about his faith. He was still a member of a local temple. He thoroughly embraced his own religion and heritage. And yet he wanted to belong to Mercy Street. "I want to join this place," he explained. "I've been in temple all my life but have never been a part of a community that brings my spirit alive like this one, and I want to join."

This blurring of the traditional divisions within religion has become commonplace at Mercy Street, and it's an issue that churches supporting recovery ministries will confront on a regular basis. This requires us to wrestle — in much the same way that observers of Jesus had to wrestle — with our preconceived notions about what it means to believe, belong, and worship within the context of a church community filled with people who come with more questions than we have answers. Churches with recovery ministries often must learn to tolerate some of the difficult tensions that arise when people of other faith traditions express interest in joining the community of Christ's followers.

People in recovery are authentic in ways that sometimes hide their sincere desire to change and be healed. They are messy, rowdy, and opinionated. They smoke too much and require a lot of coffee. But they are also spiritually hungry and will come to you prepared to wrestle with the gospel message in profound ways. These people want answers. They don't care about the denomination or theological position of the church. But they want to meet God.

4. Churches need recovery ministries, and recovery ministries need the church. It's easy to see why recovery ministries need the church. Mercy Street's primary financial donor is Chapelwood United Methodist Church. And the contribution is more than just financial. It's a covenantal commitment to the mission of Mercy Street. Chapelwood provides the meeting space on Saturday night and lends its reputation as a solid community presence to the Mercy Street cause. The organizational structure of this older, traditional Methodist church provides Mercy Street with an infrastructure capable of managing payroll, hiring staff, and accepting contributions. The church provides rooms for child care, equipment, and a natural place to turn when Mercy Street needs volunteers or community support.

But to be the church of Jesus, the church also needs the people who are looking for recovery ministries. Matt says, "I rapidly began to see that we, the church, needed them — their honesty and their dysfunction — as much as they needed the church. What most of these people needed was a church that would fully embrace their past and would support them in their spiritual journey. They needed a community that would allow them to ask as many questions as they wanted and was prepared to answer. We needed them as much as they needed us."

Recovery ministries benefit when churches are willing to risk a little confusion for the sake of reaching out to the people Jesus came to serve (see Mark 2:17). This kind of relationship benefits both the church and the recovery ministry. Yes, a commitment to a recovery ministry will always be a challenge. Faith-based recovery is still in its pioneering phase. But for those willing to take the plunge, it can be a mission field that provides endless opportunities to be wowed by the amazing grace of God.

Questions for Reflection and Discussion

1. Where have you seen grace at work recently? Describe what happened.

2. Who is the angriest person to leave your church? Why did that person leave?

3. In what ways does your church help to deal with the real pain and problems in people's lives?

4. How does your church welcome people from different cultures and make them feel a part of the congregation?

WHERE WE GO FROM HERE

> The best time to plant a tree is ten years ago. The second best time to plant a tree is today.
>
> — *Chinese proverb*

I (LIZ) WAS SITTING IN A RESTAURANT waiting to meet my friend Natalie for lunch. I watched a group gathered in the corner of the café, laughing quite loudly over a joke. Normally, this wouldn't be something I would notice or think about, but at this particular time in my life, as I listened to them laugh and saw the joy on their faces, I was reminded of my own lack of joy. I couldn't think of a single thing that anyone could do or say that would cause *me* to laugh like that. In fact, I couldn't remember the last time I had laughed. I was terribly depressed, and I didn't know why.

In the process of seeking help, I started to see a counselor. As we began to address the issue of my depression, he said this: "One thing you will need at this dark point in your life is a support system of people. I can be one of them, but you need others who can walk with you during this time."

I soon discovered how important his advice was, as my struggle with depression took a turn for the worse. I found myself questioning much of what I believed. I tried my best to make sense of my life, but there were days when feelings of darkness engulfed me. I felt isolated and confused, and I wasn't sure how God fit into what I was feeling. In fact, I wasn't sure about God at all anymore! My thoughts often spiraled downward to such depths that I feared I would never return.

But in the midst of all this, there were a couple of friends, along with my husband, who walked me through this difficult time. They listened to me when I needed to talk and wisely refrained from trying to straighten me out or fix my problems. They gave no hint of judgment or disappointment. This was important to me, because I was already carrying around a strong sense of self-condemnation and shame for feeling depressed and not having the faith to trust my way out of all this. These friends communicated compassion to me. Spending time with them gave me glimpses of rest and comfort. I had always known that it was important to have friends, but at this point, my friends were more than a pleasant addition to my life; they were necessary for my survival.

Living in the Pit

It's difficult to explain to someone who has not experienced the fear, isolation, self-abasement, and shame that can accompany times of depression, struggle, failure, and loss. As a close friend of mine, who has been a leader in recovery ministry for many years, has shared with me, the process of recovery is like trying to climb your way out of a dark pit. As you attempt to look through the darkness that surrounds you, you ask yourself, "How did I end up here? What should I do now? Will I survive? How can I ever make my way out of this pit of darkness?" You feel alone, afraid, and are without answers.

Soon someone walks up to the hole, looks down, and yells, "What are you doing down there?"

"I don't know," you reply.

"Well, why don't you get out?"

"I don't know how."

"Okay. I'm going to pray for you." He prays for you and walks on.

Although you appreciate his effort, you don't feel any better, and you're still alone in the dark.

Another person walks by. She looks in the hole and says, "Hey! What are you doing down there?"

"I don't know," you reply again.

"Why don't you get out?"

"I don't know how."

"Let me share some Bible verses with you." She shares the verses from Scripture and continues on her way.

You appreciate her effort too, but somehow it makes you feel a bit more shame.

A police officer comes along and notices you in the hole. "Hey, you can't be in that hole. It's against the law! Get out!"

"I don't know how," you respond.

So he writes you a ticket, drops it in the hole, and tells you, "You're going to have to pay for that, you know." And he walks on.

You know you shouldn't be here. You feel that your life is a poor example of faith and godliness. People have prayed for you. They've shown you the error of your ways. They have given you Scriptures. And yet you remain in this pit.

Finally, one more person calls down to you. "Hey, what are you doing down there?"

You answer once again, "I don't know."

He asks, "Why don't you get out?"

You answer with a voice laced with defeat and shame. "I want to ... I really want to ... but I don't know how."

There is a moment of silence. Then you hear a loud *thump*. You look over your shoulder. You can barely make out the dim silhouette in the darkness. You hear a voice say, "I know this darkness. I have been here too. May I go with you as you begin the climb? Having made the climb myself, I am familiar with some of the difficulties and challenges you may encounter. It will take time, there will be setbacks, but having been here myself, I have seen that there is a way out." That's when hope begins to stir. Maybe, just maybe, there really is a way out of this pit.

The pews of churches are filled with people who are stuck in the pit. They may look successful or accomplished, but on the inside they hurt. Outside the church are those who also hurt, and they have turned away from the church because the church did not make things better for them but often made things worse. Where they looked for grace, they found judgment; where they sought empathy, they found apathy; where they hoped for a lifesaver, they found an anchor that pulled them ever deeper.

But church can be different.

Redeeming Lives

Recovery is the process of redeeming lives. Recovery brings hope to places that feel hopeless and encouragement to people who are lost and confused. Recovery communicates fresh starts and new beginnings. Recovery celebrates grace, hope, and change with the expectancy that the best days of our lives are still ahead of us. Churches can be places of the healed, the healing, and the healers.

Our congregations are filled with people who need healing, as well as many who can be used by God to bring that healing to them. Sometimes we are the healers, at other times we are the ones in need of healing, but whenever we struggle through life's disappointments, losses, failures, and wounds, God can not only meet us in our pain and discouragement but also use that pain to be a qualification for ministry to others. Our struggles are the training ground for ministry, and as I learn more about the needs of people struggling with addiction, depression, and loss, I am convinced that we need to take to heart the words of 2 Corinthians 1:3 – 4: "Praise be to the God and Father of our Lord Jesus Christ, the Father of compassion and the God of all comfort, who comforts us in all our troubles, so that we can comfort those in any trouble with the comfort we ourselves have received from God."

In this passage, Paul reminds us that hurting is often a prerequisite for helping and healing. Because we ourselves have been recipients of God's compassion and comfort, we in turn have what others need — compassion and comfort. God's compassion equips us to minister to others in need, and so begins a chain reaction of healing.

Still, there are two hindrances to this chain reaction. First, there is the fear of rejection and judgment. For churches to be places of redemption and healing, we all need to know that the church is a place where it is safe to tell the truth about our lives — the good, the bad, and the ugly. This sense of safety is created and felt when the truth of our lives is met not with judgment but with compassion. Compassion is the fruit of God's gift of grace. Compassion is a merciful response to sin and failure, a suspension of judgment rooted in a humble awareness that we all stand in need of mercy. Compassion is a willingness to share in the struggle of another person, to feel what they are feeling and come alongside them in the midst of their pain. Compassion is the movement from apathy to empathy. It is the thump on the ground that says, "I've been here before, and there is a way out."

Dr. Bill Thrall explains the outworking of God's grace like this: "Grace brings us adoption into God's family, a new identity, a new life, new power, new capacity, and God's full protection — with absolutely no strings attached! But grace is much more than a theological position. Equally and simultaneously, grace is an actual environment, a realm, a present-tense reality that weaves around and through every moment of even our worst day.... Like any atmosphere, an environment of grace contains intangible, yet detectable, qualities."[32] Bill adds that as we learn how to live among others with nothing hidden, we create an environment of grace that welcomes all people into our community and accepts them wherever they are in their journey.

Despite the wide diversity of models and ministers that we've highlighted in this book, each community can be defined by a common feature: they are all places where the light of grace shines brightly and people live with nothing hidden — from themselves, from one another, or from God. Each leader has his or her own story of authenticity and grace.

- Matt Russell went in search of people who had left church, and uncovered his own addiction in the process.
- Chad Hunt grew up as a prodigal, became a preacher, and now has a son who is in jail as a result of an addiction, the very thing he is trying so hard to eradicate in his community.
- Morris Dirks dared to tell the truth. He exposed his congregation's failure to apply what was preached to their daily lives, as well as his own inability to come up with a solution to the problem.
- Jane Wolf helped to create an effective recovery ministry in her church, only to face her own son's struggle with addiction.
- Pieter Van Waarde, against the advice of his associate pastor, risked offending his congregation by beginning

a series on healing and by sharing a real, personal story from his family's past.

- Obie Bussey lives with nothing hidden, but he also embraces the blessing of God's restoration. He willingly acknowledged that he had a problem and asked for help.

- Chuck Robinson was welcomed and accepted at Henderson Hills as he struggled through his alcoholism, but his ability to minister to people today is the fruit of allowing the process of recovery to shape and mature him. Now he is empowered to minister to others who are trapped in the same pit he found himself in years ago.

Each story is different, but the common ingredient of grace weaves its way through each life and each church.

The second hindrance to a chain reaction of healing and helping occurs when churches recognize and embrace brokenness but ignore God's power for change. They have never asked the Jesus question: "Do you want to get well?" (John 5:6).

Recently I (Teresa) was hanging out with some pastors who had broken away from the more traditional church model and started their own thing. They had all come out of a buttoned-up church where it had often felt as if holiness were spelled B-E G-O-O-D, so instead they came together to create a community where it was acceptable to show up messed up. They made it a casual gathering, eliminated a lot of the rituals, and above all kept it real. Fifteen years into their grand experiment, they now find themselves asking a new question: Is it enough simply to embrace brokenness? Where's the healing? Might there be more to the story than just being honest and real with one another?

If living with nothing hidden is all there is to successful recovery ministry, then reality television would be the answer to all of our problems. But just keeping it real isn't what soothes our wounds and heals our souls. Churches must address the need to provide a safe environment for suffering while still illuminating a path toward restoration. The authors of *TrueFaced* lend their insight here: "Millions of people have yet to meet the King of Love. When they see us living in blame, shame, fear, denial, and anger, with no real answers, it confuses them. When they see us attempting to mask those dysfunctions, it tells them not to trust us — or the God we follow. When they see us focused on wounds that never heal, they conclude we cannot deal with theirs."[33]

While many recovery ministries are good at emphasizing openness, authenticity, and communicating grace to people in need, not all recovery ministries have embraced a definitive restoration model. Most seasoned practitioners know that there isn't a single formula for the process or a guarantee of success. However, those who feel called to this ministry carry in their hearts a deep belief in the possibility of both restoration and transformation. There are enough successes to let us know that God is at work in these ministries, as well as enough stories of failure and disappointment to keep us humble and dependent. Without a deep conviction that God is in the business of renovation, that he is the one who brings healing and change to lives, it would be very difficult to stay faithful to the call.

What's Next?

I (Liz) don't know a pastor whose heart cry is not, "God, give me the faith and the wisdom to lead this church in the way you desire." Every pastor wants to see the church become a place where God's grace is exhibited, where people come to know God and their lives are transformed. I know many pastors who work sacrificially, putting in long hours, investing in the lives of others. I have also met many pastors who have been disappointed and discouraged when a congregant in whom they have invested time, emotion, and prayer makes destructive choices. Many leaders give themselves to others and still end up experiencing great loss: loss of family members, loss of faith, and sometimes loss of life.

1. Begin in the Pulpit

If the senior pastor is the one with the vision for recovery, the best place to begin may be in the pulpit. When a pastor can make the ministry of recovery personal by sharing his story, he helps to introduce recovery language to the congregation, and by telling the truth about himself, he sets the stage for others to do the same.

Pastor Jorge Acevedo revealed his vision for a ministry of recovery in a simple statement that has remained Grace Church's overriding theme: "Lord, send us the people nobody else wants or sees." He said, "I do not buy into a theology that says that we are always delivered from our afflictions, but I do believe Scripture preaches that we are also in a process of recovery from the damage."

Here are four simple ways a pastor can encourage a culture of grace from the pulpit:

1. Make it personal; tell your story.
2. Make it normative through repetition; reflect the truth of your life from week to week.
3. Make it visionary; talk about your heart and passion for changed lives.
4. Make it theological; tell why you believe recovery is God's process of restoring what is broken.

2. Take Some Baby Steps

Perhaps a pastor is not yet ready to share or has not experienced the process of recovery for himself. There are other ways to influence the culture of the church that can still have a significant impact on the congregation. Dale Ryan, president of the National Association for Christian Recovery and director of the recovery program at Fuller Theological Seminary, shared that he was once talking with a pastor who was discouraged about the state of his church. It seemed to him that his congregation wasn't making the leap from head knowledge to heart change. This bothered him and caused him to doubt himself, even to question his calling. He had arranged a meeting with Dale out of his frustration and a strong desire to change his church. But the more they talked, the less convinced he became that he or his church could do the things that Dale was suggesting to him.

Dale refused to be dissuaded. "Look, start small. Can you think of one small thing you can change?"

"No."

"Here's a suggestion. Next Sunday is Mother's Day. Will you stand up and mention the holiday, express gratitude for moms, and all that usual Sunday stuff?"

"Yes."

"This Sunday, do it differently. Say something like, 'I know this is a special day for many families who are celebrating this day. I also know that some of you have mixed emotions about Mother's Day. Perhaps your relationship with your mom isn't great; maybe you don't feel like you are a good mother yourself. I just want you to know that I am aware that for some of us, this day is difficult.'"

For most churches, this would not be much of a change. But the discouraged pastor followed Dale's small, simple suggestion, and the results were astonishing. One brief mention of the possibility of a complicated life, and people began to flock to his office, sharing their stories and asking for help. Not every church needs to figure out how to start a recovery ministry, but they do need to ask how they can help their congregation experience church as a safe place to share their issues and seek solutions.

Even small adjustments in the words a leader uses can make a huge impact on the church. Dennis Newkirk of Henderson Hills Baptist Church recognized a tendency for people in the church to speak of "them out there" — referring to people who were sick and struggling with addictions — as opposed to "us in here" who have it all together. Dennis brought the language issue to the attention of the church and pointed out to them that it was this very way of thinking that led Jesus to harshly criticize the Pharisees. Here are a few simple suggestions that could shift the way you talk, changes that will subtly influence the culture of your community:

- Think through ways you can make your message more inclusive.

- Address the joys of each season, but also acknowledge the pain some may associate with certain holidays.

- Consider carefully how to avoid "us and them" language when you communicate both in the pulpit and in general conversation.

- Ask someone who is new to the faith to give you feedback.

- Develop your own glossary of recovery language.

I (Liz) was talking about the ministry of recovery with my pastor,

Tom, the other night. He had recently attended a recovery conference because he wanted to make a place within the church for some of our members who are struggling. As we talked about all the different ways the church could seek to minister to people, how it's a shift in the culture and not simply a program, and how the church can become a place of healing for people, Tom paused and said, "I'm not sure our church is really in a place to make all the changes you just described. But I do know this: that I get calls and emails from people in our congregation who confess to me about their secret addiction to alcohol. I would like to start by making a place of recovery for them."

One thing that any pastor in any church can do is this: start small. An illustration can be inserted in a sermon that helps the congregation know that their pastor hears their struggles and does not condemn them. Most churches could begin with one small group, using materials to guide the focus. Materials on both Christian recovery and codependency — the two basic starter groups that will always bring in a crowd — are available for support groups. Start a conversation. Begin with a prayer. There is no single way of bringing recovery into the life of your church. Start small, but start somewhere.

3. Listen to the People around You

As you begin a recovery ministry in your church, take some time to get to know the needs of the people in your church and your community. This helps establish a direction for you as you begin. After all, a ministry to drug addicts won't be of much help if the people in your community are struggling with alcoholism or another form of substance abuse. Matt Russell chose a unique approach to assessing the needs within his community. Matt began by interviewing people who had left the church, and as he listened to their stories, he gained insight into the needs his church was overlooking. He set up office at a coffee shop in town and spent an entire year just listening. With ears to hear and eyes to see, Matt felt that he was better prepared to minister to the real needs of real people.

Another approach is to find some individuals within your congregation who have gone through the recovery process. Jorge Acevedo made an announcement one Sunday morning and invited "the friends of Bill W.," one of the founders of Alcoholics Anonymous, to meet with him after church. Jorge knew that the reference to Bill W. would make sense only to people who were closely acquainted with AA, the twelve-step process, and the Big Book. At the meeting, he invited those who showed up to join him and meet every week for six months. Out of that initial group, they established a recovery ministry. In a similar way, Golden Gate Missionary Baptist Church started its outreach recovery ministry with the help of a deacon who happened to be a former alcoholic, fifteen years sober.

Henderson Hills Church launched the Ministries of Jesus after they conducted a survey of their city and realized there was nothing available that offered the kind of holistic ministry Jesus came to address, which includes the entire person — body, soul, and spirit. Dennis Newkirk saw that whether a person's problem is an illness or an addiction, all three dimensions of their lives are affected. The church's recovery ministry was birthed out of that desire to minister to the whole person.

4. Look for Laborers within the Harvest

If you start by tapping into the people around you, you may soon discover a rich source of equipped laborers within your own congregation. You can begin to identify people in your church by

- doing a confidential survey focused on the issues of greatest struggle. (People will not be forthcoming if they are sitting next to someone who might glance at their answers.)

- exploring what resources are available in your local community and identifying what issues are being addressed.

- asking people to tell you their stories. Listen with new ears. Consider how they might become a potential leader or attender in a recovery ministry.

- considering the background, education, and work experience of those in your congregation. There may be potential ministry leaders among those involved in the fields of counseling and social work.

- looking for those whom God has comforted and healed to be "first domino people" in the chain reaction of helping and healing others.

There are often people within your church who, through life experience, work experience, and education, are ready and waiting to move into action. Coauthor Teresa never set out to plant a recovery church, but she volunteered to be part of a team of people who valued the need for a recovery ministry. A staff that empowers its lay leaders multiplies its ability to serve others.

5. Try a Bit of Research

As churches look to develop a plan for recovery and restoration in their communities, flexibility is essential. Each year brings new discoveries and breakthroughs in the field of faith-based recovery. Effectively cooperating in the transformation process that God is doing in people's lives requires that we take risks, try new things, and work to figure out what is best for our particular situation. Even if the shoe fits, it still might not be your shoe. Here are some simple things you can do, as a leader, to educate and prepare yourself to lead a recovery ministry:

- Do some research on organizations such as the National Association for Christian Recovery to find resources and training opportunities.

- Visit local churches with a reputation for doing effective recovery ministry, and attend recovery meetings if you can.

- Look at the recovery materials that are already available. Celebrate Recovery is a great place to start. Included at the end of this book are several appendixes and a bibliography of resources for further study.

- Do a study on the twelve-step process. Understand the flow of the Twelve Steps and how they have been used in different settings.

- Develop a program that fits your culture and addresses your most obvious needs. Feel free to adapt what others have done and change materials to meet your specific needs and the culture and theology of your church. As we've said already, one size does not fit all.

Nurturing the Culture of Grace

The church service was coming to an end, and I (Liz) could tell that we were approaching the final prayer. I was a bit distracted. All I could think about was the unseasonably warm weather, and I was a bit antsy to go outside and enjoy the day. But just then, as we bowed our heads to pray, something unusual happened. With my eyes closed and my mind ticking off the minutes remaining until I could get out of the service and into the sunshine, a vision suddenly intruded on my thoughts. I saw a picture of myself embracing the woman standing at the other end of the pew.

"What a strange thing," I thought. I did not know this woman very well. We had chatted on occasion, but why would I suddenly have a picture in my mind of me holding her?

As the prayer ended, I brushed off the vision as nothing more than the result of something I had eaten the night before and began heading for the door. I glanced back and noticed that my husband was not with me. Not only was he neglecting to follow me out, but he had struck up a conversation with the husband of the woman I had just seen in my vision. Not wanting to be rude, I joined them. They were talking about their son, a young man who was finishing grad school and was about to begin a promising career. As the men continued their conversation, I turned to the woman and asked, "So tell me, how is your daughter doing?"

As soon as I mentioned her daughter, the woman's eyes focused on the floor, and I could tell something was wrong. "I'm afraid she's not doing very well," she confessed with a quivering voice.

"Has something happened to her?"

The woman paused and said quietly, with a sense of fear, "You see, my daughter has some very difficult emotional and mental issues." As she continued, I learned that her daughter was suffering from a mental illness. She spoke of the impact that mental illness can have on a family and of the decisions that brought dire and painful consequences to the entire family. She spoke of unanswered prayers and feelings of darkness and isolation. She talked about her fear and her struggling faith. She admitted that she was not too sure about God anymore. She explained that when she had attempted to bring up the subject of her daughter in the past, she had received some looks and responses that made her uncomfortable. Over time, she had decided that it was best to just keep quiet about the matter.

Had I not walked through my own time of darkness, fear, and isolation, I might also have responded in the way the others had, but as she stood there with tears welling up in her eyes, I told her of the image I'd had, during the prayer that morning, of us embracing. She began to cry, and we hugged.

Our relationship has changed over time. We don't see each other often. But on occasion we still leave a message or prayer request for each other, something that we might not share with someone else. There is a level of trust that was born of our experience that Sunday.

I do church differently these days. It's no longer primarily about how good of a preacher the pastor is or whether his sermon met my needs that day. It's not about whether the music touched my soul. More and more, it's about the people who gather with me. It's about looking for ways to nurture a culture of grace in our church, to make it a place where people can be real and honest with one another and then find hope and encouragement that God is still in the business of transforming lives. Recovery is a process. It's the process of God redeeming lives, and it's about you and me responding to his call to be a part of that process.

How will you respond today?

Alcoholics Anonymous's Twelve Steps

1. We admitted we were powerless over alcohol — that our lives had become unmanageable.

2. Came to believe that a Power greater than ourselves could restore us to sanity.

3. Made a decision to turn our will and our lives over to the care of God as we understood Him.

4. Made a searching and fearless moral inventory of ourselves.

5. Admitted to God, to ourselves, and to another human being the exact nature of our wrongs.

6. Were entirely ready to have God remove all these defects of character.

7. Humbly asked Him to remove our shortcomings.

8. Made a list of all persons we had harmed, and became willing to make amends to them all.

9. Made direct amends to such people wherever possible, except when to do so would injure them or others.

10. Continued to take personal inventory and when we were wrong promptly admitted it.

11. Sought through prayer and meditation to improve our conscious contact with God, as we understood Him, praying only for knowledge of His will for us and the power to carry that out.

12. Having had a spiritual awakening as the result of these Steps, we tried to carry this message to alcoholics, and to practice these principles in all our affairs.

Available at *http://aa.org/en_pdfs/smf-121_en.pdf* (April 10, 2010).

Celebrate Recovery's Twelve Steps and Biblical Comparisons

1. *We admitted we were powerless over our addictions and compulsive behaviors, that our lives had become unmanageable.* "I know that nothing good lives in me, that is, in my sinful nature. For I have the desire to do what is good, but I cannot carry it out" (Rom. 7:18).

2. *We came to believe that a power greater than ourselves could restore us to sanity.* "It is God who works in you to will and to act according to his good purpose" (Phil. 2:13).

3. *We made a decision to turn our lives and our wills over to the care of God.* "I urge you, brothers, in view of God's mercy, to offer your bodies as living sacrifices, holy and pleasing to God — this is your spiritual act of worship" (Rom. 12:1).

4. *We made a searching and fearless moral inventory of ourselves.* "Let us examine our ways and test them, and let us return to the LORD" (Lam. 3:40).

5. *We admitted to God, to ourselves, and to another human being the exact nature of our wrongs.* "Confess your sins to each other and pray for each other so that you may be healed" (James 5:16).

6. *We were entirely ready to have God remove all these defects of character.* "Humble yourselves before the Lord, and he will lift you up" (James 4:10).

7. *We humbly asked Him to remove all our shortcomings.* "If we confess our sins, he is faithful and just and will forgive us our sins and purify us from all unrighteousness" (1 John 1:9).

Available at *http://aa.org/en_pdfs/smf-121_en.pdf* (April 10, 2010).

8. *We made a list of all persons we had harmed and became willing to make amends to them all.* "Do to others as you would have them do to you" (Luke 6:31).

9. *We made direct amends to such people wherever possible, except when to do so would injure them or others.* "If you are offering your gift at the altar and there remember that your brother has something against you, leave your gift there in front of the altar. First go and be reconciled to your brother; then come and offer your gift" (Matt. 5:23 – 24).

10. *We continued to take personal inventory and when we were wrong, promptly admitted it.* "If you think you are standing firm, be careful that you don't fall!" (1 Cor. 10:12).

11. *We sought through prayer and meditation to improve our conscious contact with God, praying only for knowledge of His will for us, and power to carry that out.* "Let the word of Christ dwell in you richly" (Col. 3:16).

12. *Having had a spiritual experience as the result of these steps, we tried to carry this message to others and to practice these principles in all our affairs.* "If someone is caught in a sin, you who are spiritual should restore him gently. But watch yourself, or you also may be tempted" (Gal. 6:1).

Celebrate Recovery's Eight Recovery Principles

1. Realize I'm not God; I admit that I am powerless to control my tendency to do the wrong thing and that my life is unmanageable (step one). "Happy are those who know they are spiritually poor" (Matt. 5:3).

2. Earnestly believe that God exists, that I matter to him, and that he has the power to help me recover (step two). "Happy are those who mourn, for they shall be comforted" (Matt. 5:4).

3. Consciously choose to commit all my life and will to Christ's care and control (step three). "Happy are the meek" (Matt. 5:5).

4. Openly examine and confess my faults to myself, to God, and to someone I trust (steps four and five). "Happy are the pure in heart" (Matt. 5:8).

5. Voluntarily submit to every change God wants to make in my life and humbly ask him to remove my character defects (steps six and seven). "Happy are those whose greatest desire is to do what God requires" (Matt. 5:6).

6. Evaluate all my relationships; offer forgiveness to those who have hurt me and make amends for harm I've done to others except when to do so would harm them or others (steps eight and nine). "Happy are the merciful" (Matt. 5:7); "Happy are the peacemakers" (Matt. 5:9).

7. Reserve a daily time with God for self-examination, Bible reading, and prayer in order to know God and his will for my life and to gain the power to follow his will (steps ten and eleven).

Available at *http://aa.org/en_pdfs/smf-121_en.pdf* (April 10, 2010).

8. **Y**ield myself to be used to bring this Good News to others, both by my example and by my words (step twelve). "Happy are those who are persecuted because they do what God requires" (Matt. 5:10).

Understanding the Twelve Steps

ALCOHOLICS ANONYMOUS (AA) was started on June 10, 1935, by two men, Bill Wilson (Bill W.) and Dr. Robert Smith (Dr. Bob), who were both in search of freedom from alcoholism. Wilson and Smith were greatly influenced by a group of evangelical believers called the Oxford Group, and as a result, each of the Twelve Steps had its foundation in Scripture. Those twelve steps express the heart of AA's way of life. The early AA got its ideas of self-examination, acknowledgment of character defects, restitution of harm done, and working with others straight from the Oxford Group and its former leader in America, Sam Shoemaker.[34] (It was Sam Shoemaker who led Bill W. to Christ.)

The founders of AA studied God's Word and used it to order their lives. They also took the time to study their lives — taking fearless personal moral inventories — and asked God to change anything in them that was not in keeping with the character of a godly person. They dared to believe that they could live transformed lives for the glory of God, and their faith was properly placed in the One who saves and transforms.

Although the substance of the message of the original Twelve Steps remains unchanged, these principles have been adapted for a broader recovery audience that goes beyond addiction to alcohol.[35]

The Twelve Steps are a remarkable tool for self-reflection and personal growth. In the Christian community, these steps have sometimes been viewed with suspicion. They are hard work, but the by-product for many who have worked them is a life filled with freedom and love, joy, peace, patience, kindness, goodness, faithfulness, gentleness, and self-control (Gal. 5:22–23). Who among us doesn't yearn for such a life?

Step One

"We admitted that we were powerless over our problems/dependencies[36] — that our lives had become unmanageable."

We: Recovery is not a one-person job; it requires community. Although isolation is a common coping strategy when we hurt, it's highly ineffective. Community can be uncomfortable, messy, and downright annoying, but it can also be encouraging, supportive, and help us gain clarity.

Powerless: At the heart of this step is the acknowledgment that I cannot stop doing whatever I'm doing that is leading to unmanageability, nor can I maintain the choices that are positive, healing, and healthy, in keeping with the deepest desires of my heart. When all our strategies to control self and others stop working, we're ready to admit that we are powerless.

Dependencies: These are the people, places, and things that, if we are brutally honest, we do not think we could live without.

Unmanageable: This is when life is out of control. This is not about perfection but about the ability to experience a reasonably calm life without a lot of drama and chaos.

Step Two

"We came to believe that a Power greater than ourselves could restore us to sanity."

Came to believe: As the writer of Ecclesiastes points out, this belief is a messy, complex thing. That's why coming to believe is such a process! Most of us have been cheated out of our belief and the abundant life that accompanies radical believing. ("The thief comes only to steal and kill and destroy; I have come that they may have life, and have it to the full" [John 10:10].) Our past has left many of us hurt and damaged. We're in bondage to a lot of lies — misuse of religion, cultic experiences, traditions of man that run counter to God's truth — and these harmful exposures leave us scarred. It's okay to tell the truth about what we don't know or understand or trust or truly believe.

Power: In his book *Power to Choose*, Mike O'Neil says, "There's no power in something that you're supposed to believe but don't." This step requires us to get real about what we believe.

Greater than ourselves: We must break through the wall of denial and accept this truth: we haven't got the power; the power to change lies outside our limited selves.

Sanity: If we need restoration to sanity, the implication is that we are insane. Here's a popular definition I've heard repeated so many times that I don't even know its origin: insanity is doing the same thing over and over expecting a different result.

Could: This step says that God could restore us. It does not say that he is obligated to do so or that we are given no freedom to choose what we believe. But there is the possibility of restoration, and that can indeed be a very hopeful thing to consider.

Restore: Of all the key words in each of the Twelve Steps, this is my favorite. *Restoration* is an awesome word. In the Big Book (a book used frequently in Alcoholics Anonymous as a guide to sobriety), the benefits of step two are described in this way: "As we felt new power flow in, as we enjoyed peace of mind, as we discovered we could face life successfully, as we became conscious of His presence, we began to lose our fear of today, tomorrow, or the hereafter. We were reborn."

Step Three

"We made a decision to turn our wills and our lives over to the care of God as we understood Him."

This is a controversial step. If anyone ever complains about using the Twelve Steps as a tool in a recovery tool belt, this is the step they'll take issue with. Christians sometimes say these steps are too vague; others complain that AA and the Twelve Steps are too tied to Christianity. Instead of getting caught up in all the drama, consider this: " 'I know what I'm doing. I have it all planned out — plans to take care of you, not abandon you, plans to give you the future you hope for. When you call on me, when you come and pray to me, I'll listen. When you come looking for me, you'll find me. Yes, when you get serious about finding me and want it more than anything else, I'll make sure you won't be disappointed.' GOD's Decree" (Jer. 29:11 – 14 MSG).

The third step requires that we decide to trust in a God who promises all this and more. God knows what he's doing.

We made a decision: A decision frees us from the tyranny of our emotions. "Then we will no longer be infants, tossed back and forth by the waves, and blown here and there by every wind of teaching and by the cunning and craftiness of men in their deceitful scheming" (Eph. 4:14). This passage goes on to say that the outcome of a third-step decision is growth. James 1:6 says, "When he asks, he must believe and not doubt, because he who doubts is like a wave of the sea, blown and tossed by the wind."

To turn our wills and our lives over: It is a beautiful sight to behold the turning of a life and will over to the care of God. It means that what we believe will alter how we see and respond to the world.

To the care of God: He cares for us far more than we have ever cared for ourselves. When he looks at us, he doesn't see just our problems; he sees our potential. He knows what we are made of and why we were created; we were his idea. As we work these steps, we have the opportunity to learn things like this about God and get to know ourselves better too.

As we understood Him: This phrase used to confuse me. I thought it meant that we could just make up a god that pleased us. That's not what this means. This phrase is expressing the very heart of the Twelve Steps: process. The only way we can relate to God is at the level at which we understand him. Through the process of journeying along the path of the Twelve Steps, our understanding will grow.

Step Four

"We made a searching and fearless moral inventory of ourselves."

How to make an inventory: An inventory should be written down. One description of making an inventory is found in *Power to Choose* by Mike O'Neil. On pages 64–71 of the Big Book, *Alcoholics Anonymous*, you will find the original approach suggested for a fourth step. On pages 68–74 of Melody Beattie's book *Codependents' Guide to the 12 Steps*, you will find her description of the process. The most important part about this process is that you do it. As we inventory, it is important to do so with a spirit of self-acceptance, not shame. An attitude of self-condemnation helps no one; it hinders the recovery process just as profoundly as failing to admit legitimate wrongdoing. This painful step will stir up a lot of feelings, and most of us aren't very skilled at dealing with them. Asking a spiritual advocate, a mentor, or a sponsor (try to find one familiar with the twelve-step process) to help guide the process is a wise move.

Searching: It's important to write down what we really feel and do. I know that it's tempting to write down what we think we should feel and do. But presenting a false self is cheating.

Fearless: Someone famous has said that courage is not the absence of fear but the willingness to act in spite of it. We can take this step even while we feel afraid; the fearlessness is true as we are willing to do the work.

Moral inventory: "A moral inventory is a list of our weaknesses and our strengths. This inventory is something we prayerfully accomplish with God's help. It is for our benefit."[37]

Of ourselves: This is a personal evaluation. In Lamentations 3:40, we are told to examine our ways, test them, and return to the Lord. No mention is made of examining others.

Step Five

"We admitted to God, to ourselves, and to another human being the exact nature of our wrongs."

Admitted: In families with hurts, habits, and hang-ups (that includes most families), admission is sometimes viewed as a weakness. But in the right environment — having come to know the awesome, loving God of Scripture and with a loving, mature mentor guiding us — admitting our wrongdoing can be a relief.

To God, to ourselves, and to another human being: "Are you hurting? Pray. Do you feel great? Sing. Are you sick? Call the church leaders together to pray and anoint you with oil in the name of the Master. Believing-prayer will heal you, and Jesus will put you on your feet. And if you've sinned, you'll be forgiven — healed inside and out. Make this your common practice: Confess your sins to each other and pray for each other so that you can live together whole and healed. The prayer of a person living right with God is something powerful to be reckoned with" (James 5:13 – 16 MSG). Ideally, it is best to share with someone who has worked through the twelve-step process. If you don't know anyone with twelve-step experience, look for someone who is willing to be available, who listens well, and who can relate to struggles.

The exact nature of our wrongs: The most important aspect of the admission process is to eliminate secrecy. Anything we hold back will be the very thing that keeps us in bondage. It's a challenge to admit the exact nature of our wrongs. That's why it is important and very beneficial to have an experienced listener. New insights may be revealed, and we will need to add them in writing to our original inventory.

Step Six

"We were entirely ready to have God remove all these defects of character."

Entirely ready: This step is passive, in that we are preparing to ask God to remove our defects of character; it is powerful, because willingness compels us to act. We are entirely ready when we get to the point where we're willing to ask him to take us to a new place — a grand, epic adventure where we allow him to remove our defects of character.

God remove: Apart from God, we can do nothing. Only God transforms. Only God saves. This step is asking us to believe that without God's help, we can do nothing. Then prepare to accept his help.

All these defects of character: Whatever we choose to call them, character defects are those undesirable parts of ourselves that must be removed if we are going to be our real, God-created selves.

Step Seven

"We humbly asked Him to remove our shortcomings."

Humbly: Willing to be teachable, even in areas of our lives where we don't think we need instruction. Humility takes the Do Not Disturb sign off and invites God to have his way with us.

Shortcomings: Anything in our lives that keeps us from being our God-created selves. Those traits that restrict and block our ever-increasing glory and the transformation process.

Asked: Asking God to remove our shortcomings acknowledges an important truth: he's got the power and we do not.

Remove: A gradual, healing, spiritual process of transformation.

Step Eight

"We made a list of all persons we had harmed and became willing to make amends to them all."

> God does not take away life; instead, he devises ways so that a banished person may not remain estranged from him.
>
> —2 Samuel 14:14

Became: Becoming is a process. If we will be responsible to God and make the list, he will take responsibility for us and help us become willing to make amends. How this happens is a deep mystery, and it takes place in the heart. Part of trusting God to do his part is simply making the list, in spite of our reluctance and our pain.

Willing: We must prepare to accept full responsibility for our own lives and for the harm (intended or not) our choices have done to others. The previous steps help prepare us for willingness.

List: We must recall the names and faces of people we have harmed, write their names down, and consider how we've harmed them.

Harmed: Harm is caused physically (for example, injuring or damaging persons or property, financial irresponsibility resulting in loss for another, refusing to abide by agreements legally made, neglecting or abusing those in our care), morally (inappropriate behavior regarding moral or ethical issues, including fairness, doing the right thing, irresponsible behaviors at home, work, or elsewhere, ignoring the needs of others or usurping the welfare of others with our selfish pursuits, infidelity, abuse, lying, broken trust), or spiritually (failure to live out our God-created identity to the detriment of others, failure to support and encourage that same living in others). The root of harm is usually selfishness.

Amends: The process of sincerely seeking to repair the damage done. Mike O'Neil (*Power to Choose*) describes this as a two-step process: apology and restitution.

Step Nine

"We made direct amends to such people wherever possible, except when to do so would injure them or others."

Made: In step four, you took a good, hard look at yourself, and you made a list that included people you've harmed, resentments you carry, and even patterns of behavior that continue to cause harm to yourself and others. Referring back to that list helped you make your step eight list of those you have harmed. This ninth step requires that we do something with the list. Step nine requires action.

Direct: The best amends are face-to-face. Sometimes a letter or a phone call is the next best thing. Ask God to give you the discernment necessary to decide how to approach the person you have harmed. However you choose to do so, think about the other person's perspective. Don't startle them. Ask their permission to have a meeting. Accommodate them; meet in a place and at a time that is comfortable for them. Be considerate. Be aware that you are in the wrong, and the least you can do is make this situation as comfortable for them as possible. Indirect amends are appropriate for someone who is deceased or is otherwise inaccessible. Letters that are unmailed, prayers to God, or changes in behavior are all acceptable ways to make indirect amends. Don't forget to make amends to yourself; often you are the person you have harmed the most!

Amends: Mike O'Neil (*Power to Choose*) describes this as a two-step process: apology and restitution.

Apology: "I was wrong." We tend to think of an apology as "I am sorry." The problem with that sentence is its ambiguous nature. What are you sorry for? "I'm a sorry, no-good louse," "I'm sorry I got caught," "I'm sorry you're mad at me," "I'm sorry I have to deal with this," and so on. More drama doesn't make for a better apology! When we go to the shame-based "I'm sorry" place, sometimes we just fall all over ourselves and are willing to confess anything and everything for the sake of placating the person we have harmed. Making an apology isn't about confessing that which is not true. Humans make mistakes, and some of them are whoppers. Admitting that is good. But that is not the same as shame-based amends, which merely say, "Hey, I am a sorry person." A heartfelt apology will include a deeply remorseful expression of regret for harm done. Accepting responsibility for the wrong behavior is the heart of an effective apology and can be a humbling experience.

Restitution: "What can I do to make this right?" Just saying you're sorry isn't enough, nor is it enough to decide for yourself how to make things right. An apology without restitution is not amends. Sometimes restitution takes place before an apology. It is unlikely you will be given an opportunity to apologize until you show some good-faith restitution. Remember to be willing to abandon all-or-nothing thinking. Perhaps you feel that the debt, financial or otherwise, is too large to repay. You still need to ask the restitution question and proceed with restitution as best you can.

Wherever possible: Sometimes it is not possible to make direct amends. An experienced guide will help sort this step out.

Injure: An ill-conceived step nine can cause further harm. Make sure that you check your motivation. The only purpose for step nine is to right previous wrongs — your previous wrongs. If you have resentment toward the individual you harmed, delay the process. Seek counsel. Don't let this beautiful step become an opportunity to have your resentments revealed, which will cause further injury.

Step Ten

"We continued to take personal inventory, and when we were wrong, promptly admitted it."

Steps four through nine provided us with a way to clean up the messes of our past. But the truth is, messes will still happen. Step ten mercifully provides us with a way to deal with them as they occur. This is a huge blessing. Listen to what the Alcoholics Anonymous book says about step ten: "This thought brings us to step ten, which suggests we continue to take personal inventory and continue to set right any new mistakes as we go along. We vigorously commenced this way of living as we cleaned up the past. We have entered the world of the Spirit. Our next function is to grow in understanding and effectiveness. This is not an overnight matter. It should continue for our lifetime. Continue to watch for selfishness, dishonesty, resentment, and fear. When these crop up, we ask God at once to remove them. We discuss them with someone immediately and make amends quickly if we have harmed anyone. Then we resolutely turn our thoughts to someone we can help. Love and tolerance of others is our code."[38]

Continued: Step ten helps us become successful at recovery. A tenth-step inventory is continual. We're monitoring ourselves during the day.

Take personal inventory: (You may want to review the step four study guide for a more detailed description of this process.) As I've continued to inventory, I have found that God is always revealing to me new areas of potential growth. God is in the business of transforming us into our God-created selves. Over time, our inventories will change (this isn't a rehash of the past — steps four through nine took care of that).

Wrong: As we mature, we become people who can admit when we are wrong; this intentional step helps us not to forget the value of self-inventory and cleaning up our messes.

Promptly: When we're wrong and dragging our feet about making restitution, we find ourselves more defensive, easily offended, and just plain miserable. Prompt admission helps us not to make further messes of things.

Admitted it: This continues to be a vital part of the recovery process. Secrets aren't healthy. Admit our mistakes to self, to God, and to another individual (step five). Now you're ready to take this admission and use steps six, seven, eight, and nine to resolve it.

Step Eleven

"We sought through prayer and meditation to improve our conscious contact with God, praying only for knowledge of His will for us and the power to carry it out."

> This book of the law shall not depart from your mouth,
> but you shall meditate on it day and night, so that you
> may be careful to do according to all that is written in it;
> for then you will make your way prosperous, and then
> you will have success.
>
> —Joshua 1:8 NASB

Sought: Healthy relationships are like two-way streets. Two-way streets work because everybody follows the rules: driving on the correct side of the road, not crossing the yellow line, and so on. Scripture is clear. God desires and seeks relationship with his children. Healthy relationships stay healthy when we follow the guidelines. God created us, and he knows how to relate to us. He is not codependent. We must reciprocate. All good relationships are mutually satisfying; there's healthy give and take within those relationships. Step eleven guides us in the process of building an intimate relationship with God.

Prayer: Prayer is speaking with God. When one follows the disciplines of the Christ-centered Twelve Steps, two essential parts of prayer include (1) admission of our powerlessness (step one) and (2) acknowledgement of our daily choice to accept God as our higher power (step two). Furthermore, the insights we have gained in this process will drive a large part of our continued prayer by asking God to remove our shortcomings, and so on.

Meditation: Meditation is listening to God. Some believers are scared off by the term *meditation*, but do not fear! Meditation is a biblical concept. ("My meditation of him shall be sweet; I will be glad in the Lord" [Ps. 104:34 KJV].) I love Mike O'Neil's personal description of contemplative prayer: "Let your body relax, and let all the tension and all the thoughts go out, and all the preoccupations. Either meditate on a small scripture or meditate on just one or two words. I meditate on Jesus, the Holy Spirit, or Abba Father (Romans 8:15). I just think about God and try for a while in the contemplative prayer to love God. It's quite an exercise. It's pretty interesting to try to do this. Just spend fifteen minutes if you can, or at least five minutes, just trying to love God. It's quite rewarding. So I use the contemplative prayer for meditation time. My mind will wander now and then, but I just return to my beginning meditation and try to love God."[39]

Improve our conscious contact with God: Improving our conscious contact with God usurps the voices that seek to distract us from our God-created identity and purpose. We must replace the voices that historically have led us to unintentional counterproductive behaviors; nothing changes if nothing changes. This consciousness is far greater than an acknowledgment that he exists. It is about relationship. We talk; we pray and he listens. He talks and we listen — meditation.

Knowledge of His will: We can come to know and do God's good, pleasing, and perfect will. He desires this for us; often, he wants this more than we desire it for ourselves.

Power to carry it out: I don't want to mislead you. Coming to know God isn't an act of passivity. Knowledge informs our action. God has a plan and a purpose for us that involves action. But it is his plan, his power, and his resources that will enable us to accomplish his purposes. The awesome part of this process is that we can know that, ultimately, whatever God chooses for us is far more fulfilling than any plans we can think of for ourselves!

Step Twelve

"Having had a spiritual awakening, we tried to carry this message to others and to practice these principles in all our affairs."

> It's in Christ that we find out who we are and what we are living for. Long before we first heard of Christ and got our hopes up, he had his eye on us, had designs on us for glorious living, part of the overall purpose he is working out in everything and everyone. It's in Christ that you, once you heard the truth and believed it (this Message of your salvation), found yourselves home free — signed, sealed, and delivered by the Holy Spirit. This signet from God is the first installment on what's coming, a reminder that we'll get everything God has planned for us, a praising and glorious life.
> — Ephesians 1:11 – 14 MSG

The story goes like this: once we were lost; now we are found. All that is good, but that's not all of the story. There's more. Not all days will be fine. Some days we cannot live up to our potential, and find ourselves slipping back into old patterns that are destructive. The great news is that this praising and glorious life — this God who is in the business of working this purpose out in everything and everyone — is waiting for you. You are on your way to becoming a vessel of hope. You can now do for others as others have done for you. You can bring the message of hope to hurting people. The time has come for you to express your story and share with others your experience, strength, and hope.

Take a moment to prayerfully reflect. You once were ashamed, without hope, and certainly helpless. You lost some things along the way that were important to you. You lost yourself. Who you were is gone, and a new creation lives. Once upon a time, you lost your confidence and your belief in yourself and in God. But not anymore; now you're back! Experience teaches us that being back has nothing to do with being perfect. But along the journey, in good and bad times, these steps provide us with what we need to navigate life and to learn how to serve others as we travel.

Spiritual awakening: A spiritual awakening is a prerequisite for effective twelve-step work (people unfamiliar with the lingo of the Twelve Steps call this work "ministry"). My life experience has led me to conclude that a spiritual awakening occurs sometimes when we least expect it. I find that people who have spiritual awakenings possess the ability to see the world through what I like to call "God-vision goggles." Some people have dramatic moments of clarity; others experience it as a process; many say that it was in hindsight that they became aware of God's hand on their lives. For years, evangelicals have used the term *born again.* Although many scorn this phrase, I think it clearly describes what happens: an awakening in our hearts to God.

As a result of these steps: If you choose to work these steps, and really work them, then your life may change dramatically. It isn't the steps that change you; it is God. But these steps are a way to learn how to talk to God, to listen to God, and to respond to God. It is sad to meet a religious person who is not spiritual. I know this is true, because it was once true of me! I had acquired a bit of knowledge, but

I lacked the relationship with God necessary to put the knowledge to good use. I deeply desired to be God's child, but I simply didn't know how. These steps have done more to help me learn what it means to be a kid of *the* King than anything else in my life experience. But I'm not foolish enough to believe it was the steps that saved me; it was God. The steps are a tool God uses to get our attention.

Carry this message: In recovery communities, there is a phrase that describes this message: the sharing of one's experience, strength, and hope. This isn't about giving someone information, which always can be debated and debunked. Carrying the message is deeply personal; it is experiential; it cannot be refuted or denied. Others can legitimately say that they cannot relate to one's story. But each of us has a life story to share, and no one can take that away from us.

Others: Who are these others with whom we share? They are people whom God brings into our lives. Together we discuss our experiences and hopefully our solutions. ("Praise be to the God and Father of our Lord Jesus Christ, the Father of compassion and the God of all comfort, who comforts us in all our troubles, so that we can comfort those in any trouble with the comfort we ourselves have received from God" [2 Cor. 1:3 – 4].) This is God's plan for ministry. It works like this: As we grow up in our spirituality, we begin to see ourselves more accurately and develop the discernment to see others with clarity of vision too. As we move through the growing-up process, we develop life experience. Sometimes, by the grace of God, we meet people who are ready to hear a solution. This is a God thing. Frankly, many people lose hope in solutions; they believe the lie that nothing will ever change. When Scripture says that we are ambassadors for Christ, this is what that verse means. We have been sent to use our experience, strength, and hope to carry this good news to other hurting people. Often God puts people in our path with the exact same hurt that we have experienced. In Genesis, Joseph speaks of this miraculous working of God. He's been seriously mistreated in his life, but he learned through his own spiritual awakening how to rise above the obstacles and turn them into opportunities. When confronted by his former tormentors (his brothers), Joseph says this: "You intended to harm me, but God intended it for good to accomplish what is now being done, the saving of many lives" (Gen.

50:20). God is the ultimate recycler! He takes our pain and power-fully moves in and through us to bring good from evil. This process is thwarted if we haven't truly worked through our own pain. When you've truly begun to live out the solution, rather than wallow in the problem, you will find that you have morphed into one attractive individual. People will want to know what happened to you! It's impossible to share something you do not possess. Hurting people are usually extremely sensitive and perceptive, so they will know if you are not being honest. I promise you, if you have a story of hope, God will bring others into your life for you to encourage.

Practice these principles in all our affairs: What does it mean to practice? Just what it says: every day, all the time, in every situation, we use what we've learned in these steps to order our thinking, our believing, and our behaving. There's an old saying that actions speak louder than words. I can't think of a more apt phrase to remind us of the importance of living what we try to share with others. (See Phil. 4:8–9.)

Obedience is a frightening concept for most of us. We have track records that clearly indicate that this is not our strong suit. But this skill set is crucial to thriving in the midst of the twelfth step. Often-times I have asked the Lord, "How can I obey that which I don't understand? How can I obey that which I understand and feel inadequate to carry out?" Here are some principles I've learned in Scripture that help me live out my own journey.

> It is God who makes us both willing and able to fulfill his good purpose. (See Phil. 2:13; 2 Cor. 1:20–22.)

> We serve the great God who is and will; his plans cannot be thwarted. "My purpose will stand, and I will do all that I please" (Isa. 46:10). (See Isa. 46:9–11.)

> We've been given one instruction: to believe; when we take responsibility to believe, God assumes responsibility for the outcome. I can only assume that he's a big-enough God to handle my predisposed shortcomings and defects of character! (Study John 6:29; Exod. 14:14; 2 Chron. 16:9.)

> God has said he will equip us; who am I to doubt? (Read 2 Tim. 3:16–17.)

Henderson Hills' Theology of Christian Recovery

THE PRIMARY CHARACTERISTIC that differentiates Christian Recovery from other approaches to life change lies in their view of spirituality. Here are some of the major theological tenets of the Christian approach to recovery at Henderson Hills.

1. *Recovery is truly Christian only if God is part of it.* Unlike a traditional twelve-step process, this approach views God not just as a nebulous "Higher Power" but rather as the Creator of the universe who has revealed himself in the Bible. Additionally, this God is a loving God, who showed his love by sending his Son, Jesus Christ, into this fallen world to save us (John 3:16).

2. *The Word of God is the authoritative rule and guide for our recovery.* We believe there is, indeed, some objective truth in this world and that it is revealed in the Holy Scriptures (Heb. 4:12).

3. *There is a real Devil.* He is a real entity, who through the power of deception is fighting for the minds of men. Truth is therefore the ultimate weapon in the spiritual warfare of Christian recovery (John 8:31 – 32).

4. *Sin is deceptive, powerful, and addictive.* As Christian author Keith Miller states, sin (or the "control disease") is the root of all addictions and compulsive disorders (Rom. 7:15 – 25).

5. *There is a redeemer.* Jesus Christ has won the victory over sin, death, and the Devil by his death on the cross (1 John 3:8). Therefore the message of the gospel brings forgiveness and the power to experience real change in our lives through God's power (Rom. 1:16).

This appendix was adapted by Henderson Hills Baptist Church from *A Guide to Effective Rescue Mission Recovery Programs* by Michael Liimatta, director of education for the Association of Gospel Rescue Missions. Printed with permission from Henderson Hills Baptist Church.

6. *This is a fallen world.* Not only are external things warped, perverse, confused, and corrupt; believers in recovery must still contend with their own fallen natures as well (Rom. 7:21).

7. *All human beings need spiritual rebirth.* Because spiritual death is a reality, we must assume that everyone needs to experience new life from God (John 3:3).

8. *There is a significant difference between guilt and "toxic shame."* Guilt is a response of the conscience to specific sinful actions. On the other hand, destructive (or "toxic") shame is an inner sense of being unlovable, unredeemable, hopeless, irreparably flawed, incomplete, and worthless. Everyone who struggles with a compulsive disorder experiences this to some degree. The gospel provides the answer for both of these dilemmas. Confession and forgiveness heal and restore the guilt-ridden and brokenhearted. Establishing healthy relationships with God and other people helps us to accept ourselves as loved and lovable (1 John 4:9).

9. *There is a definite difference between the terms* drunkard *and* alcoholic. According to the Bible, drunkenness is a moral condition. On the other hand, alcoholism is a therapeutic condition. What separates the addict from the nonaddict is not how often they drink or how much they drink but what happens when they do drink — the loss of control (or powerlessness). Once an individual becomes addicted, he or she can never be a social drinker (Eph. 5:18).

10. *God works in processes.* Recovery is not a one-time, once-and-for-all thing; it is a process (Rom. 12:2). Recovery is not just "fixing" ourselves; rather it is gaining the tools to succeed in working out what God has already put within (sanctification) (Phil. 2:12 – 13).

11. *God works through his Spirit.* The Greek word *paraclete* is used in the Scriptures to refer to the Holy Spirit. This term means "counselor" or "personal tutor." To succeed in recovery, believers must learn to respond to God's Spirit and walk in his will for their lives (John 16:13 – 15).

12. *God works through people.* There is no more isolated and lonely person than the addict. John Bradshaw says, "The deepest wound of toxic shame is the inability to develop meaningful, intimate human relations." The message of Christian recovery is that God's grace is experienced as a process which involves intensely honest and nurturing relationships with other people. They serve as agents of his grace to unravel our woundedness and reshape our thinking (Heb. 10:23 – 25).

13. *Christian recovery is "intensive discipleship."* "Putting the cork in the bottle" (not using drugs or alcohol) is no guarantee of any lasting change in an individual's life. What addicts need is a systematic commitment to an ongoing process of personal growth. Christian recovery means gaining new tools that enable us to live a new sober life and to remove all the stumbling blocks to a life of Christian victory (2 Peter 1:5 – 11). We might also consider *recovery* as another word for what that Bible refers to as "sanctification."

14. *Repentance is more than simply confessing our sins to God.* We all must own up to our own sin if we are to experience forgiveness (1 John 1:9). Still, an additional step is necessary — repentance. The Greek word for repentance is *metanoia*, which implies a complete change of mind. New thinking comes from new attitudes that have been formed by new perspectives (Acts 3:19).

15. *"Rigorous honesty" is essential for true spirituality.* Jesus declares that the truth will set us free (John 8:32), so we must make a commitment to walk in the light (1 John 1:5 – 9).

16. *There is a "therapeutic value" to talk.* Self-revelation in a safe environment is a tremendously healing experience. Support groups provide an environment that promotes this process (James 5:16).

17. *"Grace flows freely through unclogged conduits."* Christian workers cannot bring people to a place they have not come to themselves. Therefore if we want to reach out to hurting people, we must be in the process of dealing with our own issues first (1 Cor. 11:31; 2 Cor. 4:1 – 2).

Recovery Ministry Leadership Communities: Participating Churches

IN 2005, LEADERSHIP NETWORK launched the first of five Recovery Ministry Leadership Communities. Each community was composed of ten to twelve churches that brought three to five leaders to Dallas, Texas, four times over two years. Each forty-eight-hour session included the exchange of ideas, innovation sessions, strategic planning, and celebrations, all with a view toward not just expanding their own church's ministry but also contributing to the greater knowledge base of church-based recovery. Each Recovery Ministry Leadership Community was convened and directed by Liz Swanson. Below is a list of the fifty-four participating churches. Each church has agreed to be a resource to the greater body of Christ. If you are interested in learning from those who are on the journey, please contact any one of the participating churches.

Bandera Road Community Church
San Antonio, Texas
(210) 523-9085
www.brcc.net

Big Valley Grace Community Church
Modesto, California
(209) 577-1604
www.bigvalleygrace.org

Cathedral of Faith
San Jose, California
(408) 267-4691
www.cathedraloffaith.org

Caveland Baptist Church
Cave City, Kentucky
(270) 834-8110
www.cavelandb.org

Central Christian Church
Henderson, Nevada
(702) 440-8398
www.centralchristian.com

Centre Street Evangelical Missionary Church
Calgary, Alberta
(403) 520-1208
www.centrestreetchurch.ab.ca

Christ Church of the Valley
Covina, California
(626) 859-0161
www.ccvnow.com

Christ Community Church
Omaha, Nebraska
(402) 330-3360
www.christcommunityomaha.org

Christ Fellowship
Palm Beach Gardens, Florida
(561) 799-7600 ext. 1158
www.pbgcf.org

Christ the King Community Church
Burlington, Washington
(360) 757-8989
www.ctkonline.com

Christian Assembly Foursquare Church
Los Angeles, California
(213) 489-4401
www.caeaglerock.com

Church of the King
Mandeville, Louisiana
(985) 727-7017
www.churchoftheking.com

Cokesbury United Methodist Church
Knoxville, Tennessee
(865) 693-0353
www.cclive.org

Community Bible Church
San Antonio, Texas
(210) 447-1737
www.communitybible.com

Community Christian Church
Naperville, Illinois
(630) 388-5000
www.communitychristian.org

Cross Timbers Community Church
Argyle, Texas
(940) 240-5100
www.crosstimberschurch.org

Cypress Creek Church
Wimberley, Texas
(512) 847-1222
www.cypresscreekchurch.com

Duncanville Church of Christ
Duncanville, Texas
(972) 298-4656
http://duncanvillechurch.org

Eagle Brook Church
Hugo, Minnesota
(651) 429-9227
www.eaglebrookchurch.com

East Hill Foursquare Church
Gresham, Oregon
(503) 661-4444
www.easthill.org

Fellowship Bible Church
Little Rock, Arizona
(501) 224-7171
www.fbclr.com

Fellowship Bible Church of Dallas
Dallas, Texas
(214) 739-4023 ext. 144
www.fellowshipdallas.org

First Baptist Church Woodstock
Woodstock, Georgia
(770) 926-4428
www.fbcw.org

Gateway Community Church
Austin, Texas
(512) 716-1167
www.gatewaychurch.com

Ginghamsburg Church
Tipp City, Ohio
(937) 667-4678
www.ginghamsburg.org

Golden Gate Missionary Baptist Church
Dallas, Texas
(214) 942-7474
www.goldengatembc.org

Grace Community Church
Noblesville, Indiana
(317) 580-2732
www.gracecc.org

Grace United Methodist Church
Cape Coral, Florida
(239) 573-8416
www.egracechurch.com

The Grove Community Church
Riverside, California
(951) 274-2509
www.thegrove.cc

Healing Place Church
Baton Rouge, Louisiana
(225) 753-2273
www.healingplacechurch.org

Henderson Hills Baptist Church
Edmond, Oklahoma
(405) 341-4639
www.hhbc.com

Heritage Christian Center
Denver, Colorado
(303) 369-8514 ext. 1645
www.heritagechristiancenter.com

Irving Bible Church
Dallas, Texas
(972) 560-4634
www.irvingbible.org

Lake Pointe Church
Rockwall, Texas
(469) 698-2250
www.lakepointe.org

Lakewood Church
Houston, Texas
(713) 491-1408
www.lakewood.cc

Living Hope Church
Vancouver, Washington
(360) 944-3905
www.livinghopechurch.com

Living Word Christian Center
Brooklyn Park, Minnesota
(763) 315-7010
www.lwcc.org

Mariners Church
Irvine, California
(949) 854-7030 ext. 865
www.marinerschurch.org

Menlo Park Presbyterian Church
Menlo Park, California
(650) 323-8600
www.mppcfamily.org

Mercy Street
Houston, Texas
(713) 354-4406
www.mercystreet.org

Mount Vernon Baptist Church
Glenn Allen, Virginia
(804) 270-660 ext. 123
www.mvbcnow.org

NorthStar Community
Richmond, Virginia
(804) 237-7883
www.northstarcommunity.com

Park Cities Presbyterian Church
Dallas, Texas
(214) 224-2500
www.pcpc.org

Perimeter Church
Duluth, Georgia
(678) 405-2214
www.perimeter.org

Quest Community Church
Lexington, Kentucky
(859) 277-2014
www.questcommunity.com

Richland Hills Church of Christ
North Richland Hills, Texas
(817) 281-0773
www.rhchurch.org

Saint Paul's Baptist Church
Richmond, Virginia
(804) 643-4000 ext. 269
www.myspbc.org

Salem Alliance Church
Salem, Oregon
(503) 581-2129
http://salemalliance.org

Seacoast Church
Mount Pleasant, South
Carolina
(843) 270-2054
www.seacoastchurch.org

**Thomas Road
Baptist Church**
Lynchburg, Virginia
(434) 239-9281
www.trbc.org

**Watermark
Community Church**
Dallas, Texas
(972) 718-1204
www.watermarkcommunity.org

Woodcrest Chapel
Columbia, Missouri
(573) 445-1131
www.woodcrest.org

Woodland Hills Church
Maplewood, Minnesota
(651) 324-0436
www.whchurch.org

Word of Grace
Mesa, Arizona
(480) 982-3644
www.wordofgrace.org

HELPFUL BOOKS

AA Services. *Alcoholics Anonymous: Big Book.* 4th ed. New York: Alcoholics Anonymous World Services, 2001.

Beattie, Melody. *Codependents' Guide to the Twelve Steps: How to Find the Right Program for You and Apply Each of the Twelve Steps to Your Own Issues.* New York: Fireside, 1990.

Bottke, Allison. *Setting Boundaries with Your Adult Children: Six Steps to Hope and Healing for Struggling Parents.* Eugene, Ore.: Harvest House, 2008.

Dann, Bucky. *Addiction: Pastoral Responses.* Nashville: Abingdon, 2002.

Dick B. *The Good Book and the Big Book: A.A.'s Roots in the Bible.* Kihei, Hawaii: Paradise Research, 1997.

Friends in Recovery. *The Twelve Steps for Christians.* Curtis, Wash.: RPI, 1994.

Grenz, Stanley. *Created for Community: Connecting Christian Belief with Christian Living.* Grand Rapids, Mich.: Baker, 1996.

Hart, Archibald D. *Healing Life's Hidden Addictions: Overcoming the Closet Compulsions That Waste Your Time and Control Your Life.* Ann Arbor, Mich.: Servant, 1990.

Hemfelt, Robert, Richard Fowler, Frank Minrith, and Paul Meier. *The Path to Serenity: The Book of Spiritual Growth and Personal Change through Twelve-Step Recovery.* Nashville: Nelson, 1991.

Life Recovery Bible, The. Carol Stream, Ill.: Tyndale, 1998.

Lynch, John, Bill Thrall, and Bruce McNicol. *Bo's Café.* Newberry Park, Calif.: Windblown Media, 2009.

May, Gerald G. *Addiction and Grace: Love and Spirituality in the Healing of Addictions.* San Francisco: Harper, 1988.

Moore, Greg, and Diana Moore. *Face Your Own Goliath.* Aurora, Colo.: Recovery and Redemption, 2009.

O'Neil, Mike S. *Power to Choose: Twelve Steps to Wholeness.* Antioch, Tenn.: Sonlight, 1992.

Pittman, Bill, and Dick B. *Courage to Change: The Christian Roots of the Twelve Step Movement.* Center City, Minn.: Hazelden, 1994.

Roberts, Ted. *Pure Desire: How One Man's Triumph over His Greatest Struggle Can Help Others Break Free.* Ventura, Calif.: Regal, 1999.

Ryan, Dale, and Juanita Ryan. *Rooted in God's Love: Meditations on Biblical Texts for People in Recovery.* Brea, Calif.: Christian Recovery International, 2005.

Ryan, Juanita R. *Keep Breathing: What to Do When You Can't Figure Out What to Do.* Brea, Calif.: Christian Recovery International, 2009.

Swanson, Eric, and Sam Williams. *To Transform a City: Whole Church, Whole Gospel, Whole City.* Grand Rapids, Mich.: Zondervan, 2010.

Swanson, Eric, and Rick Rusaw. *The Externally Focused Quest: Becoming the Best Church for the Community.* San Francisco, Calif.: Jossey-Bass, 2010.

Thrall, Bill, Bruce McNicol, and John Lynch. *TrueFaced: Trust God and Others with Who You Really Are.* Colorado Springs: NavPress, 2004.

Twerski, Abraham J., and Craig Nakken. *Addictive Thinking and the Addictive Personality: Understanding the Addictive Process, Compulsive Behavior, and Self-Deception.* New York: MFJ, 1997.

Urschel, Harold C. III. *Healing the Addicted Brain: The Revolutionary, Science-Based Alcoholism and Addiction Recovery Program.* Naperville, Ill.: Sourcebooks, 2009.

VanVonderen, Jeff, Dale Ryan, and Juanita Ryan. *Soul Repair: Rebuilding Your Spiritual Life.* Downers Grove, Ill.: InterVarsity, 2008.

Van Waarde, Pieter. *Building Teams That Last.* Columbia, Mo.: Academic Information Systems, 2000.

Wolf, Jane Marjerrison. *Stepping Out with Hope and Healing for a Hurting World.* Centralia, Wash.: Gorham, 2009.

NOTES

1. The Barna Group, "American Lifestyles Mix Compassion and Self-Oriented Behavior," February 5, 2007, *www.barna.org.*

2. Albert Chen, "The Super Natural," *Inside Baseball*, May 27, 2008, *Sports Illustrated online*: *http://sportsillustrated.cnn.com/2008/writers/albert_chen/05/27/hamilton0602/index.html.*

3. *www.sportingnews.com/mlb/feed/2010 – 10/2010-baseball-awards/story/rangers-josh -hamilton-named-sporting-news-player-of-the-year#ixzz15AtjB6rj.*

4. Chen, "The Super Natural."

5. *The Journey of Recovery: A New Testament* (Colorado Springs: International Bible Society, 2006), A69.

6. Dale Ryan and Juanita Ryan, *Rooted in God's Love* (Brea, Calif.: Christian Recovery International, 2005), 13.

7. Rick Renner, *Sparkling Words from the Greek: 365 Greek Word Studies for Every Day of the Year to Sharpen Your Understanding of God's Word* (Tulsa: Teach All Nations, a division of Rick Renner Ministries, 2003), 725.

8. Bill Thrall and Bruce McNicol, *TrueFaced* (Colorado Springs, Colo.: NavPress, 2004), quote of the week 12.

9. Ibid., quote 14.

10. From an unpublished manuscript by Pieter Van Waarde.

11. Pieter Van Waarde, *Building Ministry Teams That L.A.S.T.* (Columbia, Mo.: AIS [Academic Information Systems], 2000), 61 – 62.

12. Ibid., 38.

13. "Step studies" in many recovery ministries are specific support groups that utilize either the Twelve Steps adopted by Alcoholics Anonymous, the Christ-centered Twelve Steps, or even an adaptation of steps, like Celebrate Recovery's model that teaches eight principles. These studies aid the attender in working through the relevant steps of recovery and making personal applications.

14. Jeff VanVonderen, Dale Ryan, and Juanita Ryan, *Soul Repair: Rebuilding Your Spiritual Life* (Downers Grove, Ill.: InterVarsity, 2008), 116.

15. Andy Williams, "Moving Recovery Ministry out of the Shadows: Innovative Churches Learn How to Take Recovery Mainstream," Leadership Network (May 22, 2006), 8, *www.leadnet.org/resources.*

16. Bill Thrall, Bruce McNicol, and John Lynch, *TrueFaced: Trust God and Others with Who You Really Are*, Experience ed. (Colorado Springs: NavPress, 2004), 69.

17. Ibid., 59.

18. For a more thorough understanding of the twelve-step process — a tool used by many recovery ministries — see appendix A. Jane Wolf also provides an overview of the

steps in her book *Stepping Out with Hope and Healing for a Hurting World* (Centralia, Wash.: Gorham, 2009).

19. Jane Marjerrison Wolf, *Stepping Out with Hope and Healing for a Hurting World* (Centralia, Wash.: Gorham, 2009).

20. Ibid., 20.

21. Ibid., 240.

22. For more information about the Christ-centered Twelve Steps and related materials, check out *The Life Recovery Bible* (Carol Stream, Ill.: Tyndale, 1998).

23. Harold C. Urschel, *Healing the Addicted Brain: The Revolutionary, Science-Based Alcoholism and Addiction Recovery Program* (Naperville, Ill.: Sourcebooks, 2009).

24. Elizabeth Glass Turner, "Lord, Send Us the People Nobody Else Wants," *Good News: The Magazine for United Methodist Renewal* (November – December 2009), posted December 28, 2009, *http://goodnewsmag.org/2009/12/28/lord-send-us-the-people-nobody-else-wants/.* Accessed January 28, 2010.

25. Jorge Acevedo, "Lord, Send Us the People Nobody Else Wants or Sees! Developing a Heart for the Poor and Broken," *Circuit Rider* (November – January 2009 – 10), 7, *www.umph.org/pdfs/circuitrider/u201Lsup.pdf.* Accessed January 27, 2010.

26. Steve Harper, *The Way to Heaven* (Grand Rapids, Mich.: Zondervan, 2003), 121.

27. Grace United Methodist Church, *www.egracechurch.com/cape-coral-campus/about/who-we-are/strategy/* (March 16, 2010).

28. Available at *http://en.wikipedia.org/wiki/List_of_shopping_malls_in_the_Dallas%E2%80%93Fort_Worth_Metroplex* (April 17, 2010).

29. Christine Wicker, "Renowned Pastor C.B.T. Smith Retiring after 45 Years," *Dallas Morning News* (April 12, 1997).

30. Matt Russell, "How a Jewish Drunk Challenged My Idea of the Church: Toward an Ecclesiology of Recovery," *www.nacronline.com/misc-articles* (February 10, 2010).

31. David Wenham, *The Parables of Jesus* (Downers Grove, Ill.: InterVarsity, 1989), 159.

32. Bill Thrall et al., *TrueFaced Experience Guide* (Scottsdale, Ariz.: Leadership Catalyst, 2004), 69 – 70.

33. Spoken by Bill Thrall during a TrueFaced event.

34. *Alcoholics Anonymous Comes of Age* (New York: Alcoholics Anonymous World Services, 1957), 199.

35. For an easy comparison of both the adaptation and the Twelve Steps of Alcoholics Anonymous, both may be found in *The Life Recovery Bible* (New Living Translation), 2nd ed. (Carol Stream, Ill.: Tyndale, 1998), A6, A8.

36. Many first steps will mention a specific malady, like "alcohol," but within the framework of a recovery ministry. Keeping it general is sometimes helpful.

37. Friends in Recovery, *The 12 Steps for Christians* (Curtis, Wash.: RPI, 1994), 71.

38. *Alcoholics Anonymous: The Story of How Many Thousands of Men and Women Have Recovered from Alcoholism* (New York: Alcoholics Anonymous World Services, 2001), 84.

39. Mike S. O'Neil, *Power to Choose* (Nashville: Sonlight, 1992), 170.

About the Leadership Network Innovation Series

Leadership Network's mission is to accelerate the impact of 100X leaders. These high-capacity leaders are like the hundredfold crop that comes from seed planted in good soil as Jesus described in Matthew 13:8.

Leadership Network...

- explores the "what's next?" of what could be.
- creates "aha!" environments for collaborative discovery.
- works with exceptional "positive deviants."
- invests in the success of others through generous relationships.
- pursues big impact through measurable kingdom results.
- strives to model Jesus through all we do.

Believing that meaningful conversations and strategic connections can change the world, we seek to help leaders navigate the future by exploring new ideas and finding applications for each unique context. Through collaborative meetings and processes, leaders map future possibilities and challenge one another to action that accelerates fruitfulness and effectiveness. Leadership Network shares the learnings and inspiration with others through our books, concept papers, research reports, e-newsletters, podcasts, videos, and online experiences. This in turn generates a ripple effect of new conversations and further influence.

Launched in 2006, the Leadership Network Innovation Series presents case studies and insights from leading practitioners and pioneering churches that are successfully navigating the ever-changing cultural landscape. Each book offers *real* stories about *real* leaders in *real* churches doing *real* ministry. Readers gain honest and thorough analyses, transferable principles, and clear guidance on how to put proven ideas to work in their individual settings. Real stories, innovative ideas, transferable truths.

Leadership Network is a division of OneHundredX, a global ministry with initiatives around the world.

To learn more about Leadership Network, go to *www.leadnet.org*.

To learn more about OneHundredX, go to *www.100x.org*.

Leadership Network Innovation Series

Real Stories.
Innovative Ideas.
Transferable
Truths.

How can you fulfill your calling as a pastor or church leader and help your church experience vitality? **Learn from those who have gone before you.**

Launched in 2006, the Leadership Network Innovation Series presents case studies and insights from leading practitioners and pioneering churches that are successfully navigating the ever-changing streams of spiritual renewal in modern society. Each book offers *real* stories about *real* leaders in *real* churches doing *real* ministry.

The Big Idea
Dave Ferguson, Jon Ferguson & Eric Bramlett
Confessions of a Reformission Rev.
Mark Driscoll
Dangerous Church
John Bishop
Deliberate Simplicity
Dave Browning
Ethnic Blends
Mark DeYmaz & Harry Li
Leadership from the Inside Out
Kevin Harney

The Monkey and the Fish
Dave Gibbons
The Multi-Site Church Revolution
Geoff Surratt, Greg Ligon & Warren Bird
A Multi-Site Church Roadtrip
Geoff Surratt, Greg Ligon & Warren Bird
Servolution
Dino Rizzo
Sticky Church
Larry Osborne
The Surge
Pete Briscoe with Todd Hillard

With the assistance of Leadership Network — and the Leadership Network Innovation Series — today's Christian leaders are energized, equipped, inspired, and enabled to multiply their own dynamic kingdom-building initiatives. And the pace of innovative ministry is growing as never before.

Learn more at www.InnovationSeries.net

Leadership Network Innovation Series

Dangerous Church

Risking Everything to Reach Everyone

John Bishop

Dangerous churches are willing to put everything on the line for the one thing that matters
most: reaching lost people. Through probing
questions and amazing stories of God's grace,
John Bishop challenges church leaders to em-
brace what matters most to the heart of God, whatever the cost.

Most churches gravitate to what is safe and familiar. Church leaders
who take risks are bound to fail, and fear drives us to continue in our
comfortable but ineffective patterns.

But reaching out to a lost world was never meant to be easy.

Jesus promised his followers that they would have trouble in this
world. Dangerous churches are churches that are willing to risk everything
— comfort, safety, and the security of the familiar — for the sake of the one
thing that matters most: reaching out to people who may spend eternity
separated from the God who created them.

God wants us to live on the edge of our margins, walking by faith
and not simply following scripted methods or programmed patterns.
Dangerous Church takes us back to the book of Acts and reminds us that
the heartbeat of the church is found not in agendas or human plans but
in pursuing the mission of God and reaching out to a lost world. Learn
what can happen when church leaders abandon their fears and begin to
live a dangerous faith.

Dangerous Church is part of the Leadership Network Innovation
Series.

Learn more at www.InnovationSeries.net